BETTER THAN A TURKISH PRISON

WHAT I LEARNED FROM LIFE IN A RELIGIOUS CULT

SINASTA J. COLUCCI

HYPATIA PRESS

Published by Hypatia Press in the United States in 2019

ISBN: 978-1-912701-66-7

Cover design by Claire Wood

www.hypatiapress.org

AUTHOR'S NOTE
THE SUBJECTIVE WORD OF MEN

I want to begin by giving credit where credit is due. Much of the knowledge that I currently possess is esoteric in nature. It is the direct result of having been indoctrinated into a religious cult, known as The Twelve Tribes Communities. For nearly eight years, I was entirely immersed in their culture, hearing their teachings and learning their theology, which itself is the result of decades of councils which regularly took place between the community's most intelligent men and rarely women (sometimes women contributed to these councils, but men were ultimately the leaders). These councils aimed to interpret the Holy Bible, and apply it to the community, using it to dictate the lives of each individual member of the cult. They also studied religious history and used it to strengthen their narrative. Though I am now my own man, free from this cult's authority, I feel it is only fair to acknowledge that this book would not have been possible without them.

Whether one believes the Bible is the inerrant word of God or not, the fact remains that it is a beautiful work of literature that has a way of leaving its mark on people. It is filled with poetry, wit, humor, sarcasm, and historical significance. I would recommend it to anybody who has even the slightest interest in religion or world history, as there is a great deal that can be learned from what is written in the various books of the Bible.

Having said that, there are a few misconceptions that should be understood before you can fully understand these works:

First off, it is not one book, but a collection of 66 different books, written by about 40 different authors[1]. Consider this when reading Revelation 22:19.

"…and if anyone takes away from the words of the book of this prophecy, God will take away his part from the tree of life and from the holy city, which are written in this book."

Was this a warning for anyone who takes away from the words of the Bible? The whole Bible? All 66 books? Remember, it wasn't one concise book at the time John wrote the book of Revelation, but rather, there were many different books, which were considered holy. So, it is not likely that John knew he was writing the last book of the Bible when he penned these words in Revelation.

People like to quote the Bible in 'Olde' English, but the most recent book of the Bible was completed at least about 500 years (and at most, about 1,000 years) before the English language was created.[2,3] The original Bible (referring to all 66 books, both old and new testaments) was written in three different languages: Hebrew, Aramaic, and Greek.[4] Having a basic understanding of these languages is part of the key to understanding the Bible. The hard 'J' sound did not exist in any of these languages. The first book to make a distinction between the letter 'J' and the letter 'I' in the English language was Charles Butler's <u>English Grammar</u>, written in 1633. This was about 22 years after the King James version of the Bible was completed, and over 100 years after William Tyndale translated the New Testament and part of the Old Testament into English.[5] So then where does the name 'Jesus' come from? Think about this as you read Acts 4:12.

"Salvation is found in no one else, for <u>there is no other name</u> under heaven given to mankind by which we must be saved."

We'll revisit the subject of language and of the Savior's name later. I use it as an example here because it is important to note before reading the Bible in the English language, that you are not reading one book in its original form, but one that has been modified throughout history. The Bible is made up of multiple books, written by multiple authors, being displayed in a language other than the language they were originally written in. I would also advise that you do not read it as if it were "the objective word of God", as many denominations of Christianity would have you do. It would more accurately be described as "the subjective word of men." While it has great historical significance, I do not view the Bible as a history book, nor a moral guide book, but rather as a collection of stories, concepts, and poems, which can help us gain an understanding of the men who wrote it, and the times they were living in.

By now, you may have guessed that I am an atheist, which was the second most negatively perceived religious group in America following Muslims, according to a 2017 Pew Research Center survey. The difference between the two groups was only two points on a scale of 1-100. Jews took the number one spot for the most positively perceived group with 67 points, followed by Catholics with 66, Mainline Protestants with 65 and Evangelical Christians with 61. Atheists scored 50 points and Muslims with the lowest score of 48. No religious group received a perfect score of 100.[6]

I currently reside in Central Lake, Michigan. The overwhelming majority of Central Lake's residents are Christian. To be clear, I do not hate people based on their religious affiliation, so if you ask me if I hate Christians, I'll tell you, unequivocally, that I do not. In fact, there have been many people who have helped me during difficult times in my life who were likely motivated by their Christian faith. Much of what I have to say about the religion and its bloody history is unrelated to my opinion of Christians in general, and is especially unrelated to modern Christians. Since most of my daily interactions are with Christians, I am often asked, when the subject comes up, why I became an atheist. Some might ask that question hoping to perform their godly duties of converting me, but I think a lot of people have a genuine curiosity, and some are legitimately concerned for my soul. I do not get offended by this, as many atheists do. I see this as a natural human inclination towards compassion. However misplaced that compassion may be, it is still legitimate and we atheists should recognize and appreciate that before we respond to such inquiries. That way we will (hopefully) respond appropriately. Whatever the motive for asking it, the question of how I became an atheist is never easy to answer. This is not only due to the personal nature of such a question, but it would also be impossible for me to give a complete answer. Even so, this book is an attempt to do just that.

CONTENTS

1. Anything but Godly 1

2. Torn 21

3. A Blossoming Myrtle Tree 60

4. Abra-Cham 90

5. A Farmer's Destiny 116

6. A Young Sprout in a Rocky Place 148

7. Controlling my own Destiny 172

8. Culture, Racism, and Personal Preference 193

9. The Size of the Universe 215

10. Religion Versus Morality 224

11. I am a Believer! 247

I

ANYTHING BUT GODLY

To be fair, I didn't start off as a Christian. I had no religious affiliation growing up, so the question of how I "became" an atheist isn't about how I fell away from the Christian faith, so much as how I learned about Christianity in the first place, and how my current position as an atheist has become so solidified. I was born in Detroit, MI in 1984. My father is very religious and always has been. He describes himself as a "Rasta man," rather than a "Rastafarian." His religion is uniquely his and seems to stem from his upbringing as a Jehovah's Witness, with a blend of Rastafarianism, an apocalyptic outlook on life, and a deep-seeded narcissism that causes him to imagine himself as the king of the biblical tribe of Benjamin. My father didn't raise me though. I didn't learn all this about him until after I met him at the age of 19. I was raised by my mother, who could best be described as a free-spirited hippie.

In 1984, Detroit, MI was a large and rapidly shrinking city and

Redding, CA was a small town that was growing fast. My entire family was from Detroit, but two of my uncles, who were carpenters, found work in Redding and my mother decided to follow them out there, along with my five-year-old sister and me. I was only three months old at the time. My mother says that her decision to move us out to California was motivated by a desire for us to grow up in a safe and healthy environment. I've asked my father why he decided to stay in Detroit instead of coming with us to Redding, and he told me this story about how my mom threatened to call the Shasta County Sheriff's Department on him if he tried to follow us out there, and how they were racist and would have shot him if he'd have shown up. Apparently moving to Redding wasn't only about our health and safety. By the time my mother made this decision, she had already decided she wanted to be far away from my father and to never see him again. To this day, she never has. I wonder: If my mother actually thought the officers in Redding were really so racist that they would have shot a black man on the spot, just for showing up at someone's door, how safe did she think we'd be there (me being mixed-race)? Sadly, she's almost entirely senile now. She is also suffering with Huntington's disease. For these reasons, I cannot understand most of what she says, otherwise I would ask her.

Indeed, racism did play a major role in my upbringing. I couldn't have been much older than four years old when my mother taught me about Nazis and the KKK, and how they would kill people who have skin like mine. I used to have nightmares about it, and even experienced a few hallucinations. I have sickle cell anemia, and would often experience intense pain. Until I was diagnosed, at the age of eight, nobody knew the reason for this pain, and I did not receive any medication for it, so when it became particularly severe, I would hallucinate. On one such occasion, late at night, I thought I saw a man wearing a white Klan hood, glaring at me through the window from outside. At a very young age, when I was still in preschool, I was consciously aware of my being different from all the other kids. Redding is primarily white, and was probably more so back in the late 1980's. I don't remember being made fun of or mistreated at such an early age, but I do remember an incident where I decided to scrape my arms vigorously with some tree bark hoping to make my skin look whiter. My mother, who also happened to be a teacher at the preschool I went to, came up to me and asked me what I was doing. When I told her, she sat down on the ground with me and spoke to me about how I should be proud of my "Native American heritage."

If you're a little confused right now as to what my actual heritage is, that's totally fine. I was a thoroughly confused child. I'm a mix of African, various European nationalities, and Cherokee. My full name is Sinasta Joseph Ukiah Colucci, but my mom just called me "Ki." From what I've heard, both of my parents named me, and they wanted me to be proud of my Native American heritage in particular, so that is where the names 'Sinasta' and 'Ukiah' came from. Both are

3

Cherokee.

I spent a large portion of my childhood thinking that my dark skin was a result of my Native American heritage, and I wasn't taught much about my African American heritage. I was enrolled in Indian Education when I was in the fourth grade. I had been held back from kindergarten until I was six years old, so I would have been ten years old when I started fourth grade. Therefore, it would have been the fall of 1994 when I witnessed actual racism from the Shasta County Sheriff's Department.

As of this writing, it has been 23 years since this incident occurred. It is important to keep that in mind before judging the present-day Shasta County Sheriff's Department. The history of relations between the local Native American tribes of Shasta County and the white settlers goes back to the 1800s. The Winnemem Wintu Tribe had been recognized by the federal government since 1851, but as of 1985 they were no longer recognized as a tribe. They had to relinquish much of their land with a treaty in 1851 and were confined to a small area along the Sacramento River Valley. They were "relocated" when the Shasta Dam was built in 1985. Everything the Winnemem tribe had was bulldozed, then flooded, with the creation of Lake Shasta. Since they were no longer federally recognized, they could not receive any assistance from the government, and the land that had been allotted to them prior to 1985 was taken from them.

This and many other tragedies, such as disease, depletion of resources, and intentional poisonings, caused the natives of Shasta County to develop some resentment towards the European American settlers.

In the fall of 1994, while enrolled in the Indian Education program, I had marched in a parade which ended at the local middle school, where I delivered a speech. Afterwards, I met up with some friends from the program and we went to the park across the street. We were playing at the playground when we saw a fight break out between a white man and a Native. Both were clearly drunk. Soon after the fight started, two squad cars pulled up. A female officer and three male officers jumped out and quickly broke up the fight. They handcuffed the Native man and let the white guy go. We watched as he staggered across the park. Once handcuffed, the Native was thrown face-down on the concrete. A couple of the male officers beat him in the back with their clubs and the female officer pulled his head back by his hair and emptied a can of pepper spray in his face. They threw him in the back of one of their cars and drove off.

I was stunned by this event, and from that time on I had been deathly afraid of being beaten or killed because of how I look. I couldn't think of any explanation for what happened other than blatant racism. All four officers were white. The white guy, from what my friends and I could see, was just as guilty as the Native. In hindsight, I realize that there could have been other factors. Perhaps the Native had a warrant out for his arrest and the white guy had no priors. But then again, why would they let him just walk off? They had two cars. Could they not have given him a ride home in one of them rather than have him walk through a park full of children in his agitated and intoxicated state? It just doesn't add up. Regardless of why it went down the way it did, that incident had a significant effect on my outlook on life, and even affected how I perceive religion. Put simply, it just wasn't fair.

For the most part, I did have a peaceful upbringing. I was called names a few times, from people who couldn't figure out what race I was. I was called "Sand Nigger," which I guess is supposed to be a slur against Arabs. Some called me "Wetback" or "Beaner"—slang for Mexican. And a few times I was called "Nigger" or simply "dirty half-breed." People couldn't figure it out, but they knew for sure they didn't like my skin color. I grew paranoid that everybody in Redding hated me and that it was just a matter of time before a mob of angry white people decided to grab me and hang me on a tree. Fortunately, I was never physically attacked.

In high school, I used to get into political arguments with people. I don't recall ever having a religious debate. It was usually political in nature, because most of the students were conservative-leaning and

I was liberal. The only incident I can remember that got out of hand was in a geometry class. I'm pretty sure the teacher was just lazy and really didn't give a fuck, or maybe he agreed with the students, but either way, it got way out of hand. Some of the students in that class thought I was gay, so they used to mock me quite a bit. I never told them I wasn't gay, because I didn't think that should matter. In my mind, they shouldn't have been treating me badly if I was gay, so why should I have told them I was straight? One time, as we were having one of these arguments, one of the guys came up behind me and pulled my pants down, boxers and all, while I was standing in front of the entire class. I quickly pulled them back up, but one of the girls in the class made a comment about the size of my (flaccid) penis, and they all proceeded to laugh and mock me for it. To this day, I still don't know how to calculate the area of an isosceles triangle, but I do know that I don't like gay bashers!

It was also in high school that I picked up my first Bible. Someone was handing these little Bibles out in front of the school. It was this little, orange-covered book. It had the New Testament, Psalms, and Proverbs. I used to read it at night. I wasn't sure what my mom would think about it, so I didn't tell her. I remember one time, it was like this miniature religious experience. I was reading my little Bible with a flashlight, and the light suddenly went out. I prayed, and it came back on! Miraculous! Since then I've had plenty of experiences with cheap flashlights that have loose batteries inside. The light will go out, but all it takes is to jiggle it a little and it comes back on. But at the time I was pretty impressed by this miracle and I thanked Jesus, even though I had never been to church and didn't really know who Jesus was or most of what he said, or actually stood for. I knew very little of religion in general at that time.

As a teenager in the late nineties, I was fascinated with end-times prophecy. There was a lot of talk about the end of the world around the turn of the millennium, and I had picked up this book about Nostradamus. There were plenty of these books written in the nineties with all sorts of theories about what exactly would take place based on Nostradamus' writings. The one I read theorized that a comet would appear in the sky during the solar eclipse of August 1999, and that it would cause a global panic. This comet was supposed to appear as big as the sun in the sky, but it wouldn't directly hit the earth. Instead, the earth would pass through the comet's tail, which would result in an onslaught of large meteors. These impacts would bring about a chain of events that would lead to World War III, the battle of Armageddon, and ultimately the return of Jesus. So, naturally there were plenty of biblical references in this book and it put enough fear in me to want to be one of God's chosen ones so that I wouldn't have to burn in hell for eternity.

I had become so obsessed with end-times prophecy, and so drawn to Christianity because of it, that at one point I even worked up enough nerve to ask my mother if we could go to church. She obliged and drove me to a Catholic church on the other side of town (we passed plenty of other churches along the way, but for some reason she decided to drive to the Catholic church). As she drove up the long driveway and pulled into the packed parking lot, I noticed the people getting out of their cars and walking towards the church's large double doors and I saw a lot of kids from school that I didn't get along with. I'm not sure why I didn't expect that, as if the church would only have godly parishioners that I somehow had never encountered before—people that were agreeable and wouldn't fight with you, call you gay, and pull down your pants. But no, it wasn't saints that I saw going into that church. It was the same people who I'd see the rest of the week, acting anything but godly. My mother asked me if I still wanted to go in and I said, "no" and we drove back home. I'm thinking she might have been relieved. Knowing her, she probably agreed to drive me to a church, because she felt guilty about keeping me from choosing whichever religion I wanted to follow, but I'm sure she had no desire to go into that church.

I left Redding at the age of eighteen. I haven't been back since. I was invited to move in with an old family friend in Ann Arbor, MI. I had been friends with her son, who was the same age as me. I'd see him whenever we would visit our relatives in Detroit, and they'd come visit us in California sometimes. I accepted the invitation to live with them and completed my final year of high school there. There's a lot

I could say about that year in Ann Arbor. What I took away from my experiences there, more than anything, is that it feels better to work and provide for yourself than it does to mooch off other people. It was also during this time that I got to see the stark contrast between how wealthy and poor people live in America. Growing up, I had very little interaction with wealthy people. When I moved to Ann Arbor, I was still poor, but a lot of the new friends I made were rich. I had been invited to stay at one guy's house a few times and it was the biggest house I'd ever seen, let alone stayed the night in. It was a bit of a surreal experience for me, because at the time I was living out of a suitcase.

The family friend I stayed with ended up getting evicted a few months after I moved in. She was a high school teacher in her fifties. She had lived in the same apartment for nineteen years, but was considering buying a house. When it came time for her to pay the lease for the next six months in her apartment, she decided not to, because she was expecting to use that money for the down payment on her new house. Unfortunately, she was not able to get the house on time (I think a few deals had fallen through at the last moment) and we ended up having to move in with her friends. Her son had left for Europe to study abroad, so it was just the two of us, moving from one friend's house to another each week in an attempt to avoid overstaying our welcome. I don't think it worked though. I got the sense that people just wondered why I was there in the first place and it was just awkward feeling like such a moocher. I spent a lot of time looking for work after school, but I also looked like I was twelve, and no one wanted to hire a twelve-year-old.

As soon as I graduated, I was eager to find work. My sister was living in Northern Michigan at the time. My sister had a different father than me, but we have the same mother and we grew up together. Her father, Dan, owned a farm in Northern Michigan and she'd go stay with him from time to time. At this time, she had a job at a resort there and she mentioned to me that they were hiring. She offered for me to stay with her at her father's house and said I could work through the summer at the resort. It sounded like a good idea to me, so I went with her (much to the relief of the generous folks in Ann Arbor).

My plan was to work through the summer, save up some money, and then start college in the fall. I wanted to be a history teacher, because I'd always been good at history in school. I figured financial aid would cover tuition and I'd be fine. Well, I did end up getting a job at the resort shortly after moving up north with my sister. It was a night shift job, washing dishes. I'd ride my bike to and from work and during the day I'd take care of the farm animals. Dan also had two younger kids, so I'd take care of them too. I was tired all the time, but it was rewarding to feel like I was contributing to the household after the year I'd just had, feeling like a moocher all the time.

Another thing about Dan (my sister's dad), was that he was a potter. He was a passionate artist. He'd teach contra dancing and would also exhibit his pottery at local fairs. Dan had a very exuberant personality and was a bit of a local hero. So, it wasn't surprising when a few artists from Detroit sought him out to get some inspiration. They'd certainly come to the right place, because Dan was an inspiring man! The three artists were Charles, Kwame, and Ras Kente. Charles was a painter, Kwame was a sculptor, and Ras Kente was a musician, who had apparently had a few jam sessions with some very famous people. They all came to see Dan while I was still staying with him. We treated them to all the sights. Dan took them out on his boat, and I cooked a nice butterflied coconut shrimp meal for everybody. I always enjoyed cooking and even considered culinary school. I don't recall what the side dishes were, but they must have been good, because the meal had apparently made an impression.

The three artists left after one week, but they said they'd be back soon. When they got back down to Detroit, they met up with their friend, who was going by the name of "Joshua" at the time. They started telling him about their time up north, about Dan and his farm, and Joshua told them that Dan sounded familiar, like someone he'd met before. Then they told Joshua about me and my cooking. I was going by the name "Ukiah," and as soon as they said it, Joshua apparently took on this really intense look and started shaking. He said, "Ukiah? That's my son!"

Meanwhile, I was pushing myself pretty hard that summer, doing much more physical activity than I had been used to. When we had taken the artists out on Dan's boat, we all went swimming, but this wasn't a good idea with my condition. When you jump into cold water on a hot day, your blood vessels constrict. When you have sickle cell anemia, the sickle-shaped cells get trapped in your capillaries when your blood vessels constrict, causing what doctors call a "pain crisis." I ended up with severe chest pain, but I kept going to work. I continued to haul five-gallon buckets of water to the horses and cows, rode my bike to and from work every night, working eight-hour shifts, until the pain reached an uncontrollable point. Then I had a nightmare of a shift.

I didn't have any prescription medications at this time, so I took a handful of ibuprofen, which doesn't do anything for sickle cell pain, so I kept taking more. When I showed up for work, the restaurant, including the banquet hall, was packed. Also, none of the other dishwashers had shown up. There would normally be three of us working. I remember being far behind schedule, just starting on the cooking dishes when I should have normally been clocking out, but I felt like I needed to keep going. I also remember that every time I'd have to lift the baking pans up onto the racks to dry, it felt like my chest was ripping open. I was just finishing up with the pots and pans when the day crew, who I had never met before, showed up and started cooking. They kept bringing more dirty dishes to me and I didn't know when I could stop. Finally, the day crew manager came to me and told me I should probably just go home. I rode my bike home, laid down for a couple hours, and then Dan's wife asked me to watch the kids and take care of the animals. Looking back, I don't know why I kept going and did all my chores that day, but it wasn't until mid-day that I finally admitted that I needed to go to the hospital. I didn't show up for my dishwashing job again.

It was only about two weeks before I was to start college in Detroit. I had been bedridden for eight days at the hospital in Traverse City. Shortly after my release from the hospital, those three artists came back up for an art fair and they told us about my father. They also offered me a ride back down to Detroit with them and I accepted. I had stayed the night at Ras Kente's house, and the next morning he handed me his phone and said I had a call. When I picked up the phone and said, "Hello," my dad started talking. He didn't stop for about another hour. It was an odd experience listening to him though, because he was a stranger to me, and yet it was like listening to my own voice. He had attempted to defend himself for not having been a part of my life, telling me his side of the story of what had transpired between him and my mother 20 years prior.

My father came and picked me up from Ras Kente's house in Highland Park and brought me to his place on the east side of Detroit. He said it had been "really mystical" the way we had been

14

brought together. He said that when he was with my mother, she took him to meet Dan. He remembered riding one of Dan's horses. Dan later told me the same story, about seeing this "huge, muscular black man with long, flowing dreadlocks, riding an Arabian horse—bareback, and at a full gallop." Indeed, it was an interesting coincidence that I met my own father through my sister's father, and that the two had only met once before.

I stayed with my father for a few days. Like me, he too was obsessed with the end of the world. He told me his own apocalyptic visions and predictions for the future. My father was convinced that the world, as we knew it, would come to a violent end in the year 2012. But he also thought that the Messiah would come back at that time and setup a kingdom on Earth and would appoint kings to rule over each of the tribes of Israel (my father was to be the king of the tribe of Benjamin). As improbable as it all sounds (especially looking back, now that 2012 has come and gone), I believed most of what he told me. He also mentioned at one point, that he felt like "a commune where they grow their own food would be a safe place to be."

After spending a few days with my father, he gave me a little cash (he grew and sold marijuana for a living), and he helped me move into my dorm room at Wayne State University. As it turns out, my plan of having college paid for by financial aid and becoming a history teacher was not as solid as I thought. I was able to get tuition and some of my living expenses paid for by a grant and a loan that I had taken out, but it was the dorm's mandatory meal program that really did me in (that and my lack of motivation). The meal program was really expensive, and I was automatically enrolled in it. I couldn't pay for it, and eventually I was kicked off the meal program, which meant that I still had to pay for it, but I could no longer eat in the cafeteria. At that point, rather than ask for help, I just decided not to eat (I was a very proud individual back then).

On occasion, my mother would mail me some money and my father would also help from time to time. I would spend their money on food, but I would go out to eat, since I was not allowed to cook in the dorm room and was apparently not smart enough to shop for inexpensive food that didn't need to be cooked. I was somehow able to get through the first semester of college. That winter, in February, right before the Super Bowl, I had gone a couple days without eating. Then my aunt invited me to watch the game with my cousins (her sons). That weekend I feasted on all sorts of high-fat, delicious junkiness! The next week I had another sickle cell crisis.

I called my father and he brought me to his house. He fed me meals which consisted primarily of leafy green vegetables and beans, or tofu, which is also beans, but fermented. He gave me a joint to smoke for my pain. He said it was medicinal. Unfortunately, it did not work. After a few days spent in agony on my father's couch (not because of the food, but because of the pain), I asked to see a doctor. "Doctors are wicked people!", he proclaimed. "What are they going to do to help you?"

I said, "Well, the first thing they're going to do is draw my blood."

"Drawing blood is wicked!" he said. "They're like vampires!"

Eventually he did drop me off at a clinic near the university campus and drove off. The sign on the door of the clinic read, "By appointment only." There was a hospital nearby, but I didn't want to go to the ER, so I ended up walking the 5 blocks in the cold, back to my dorm room. Later that night I called my aunt. She was very concerned and said that I should go to a hospital. I told her I didn't want to and that the pain was mostly in my legs (I had also been experiencing a lot of pain in my gut). "What am I going to do, tell them my legs are hurting?" I asked. "No, you have sickle cell, and that's what you need to tell them," was her response. She drove me to a hospital, and as it turned out, I was not only experiencing a sickle cell crisis, but also a gallbladder infection.

After this incident, my family (on my mother's side) became very concerned. They provided me with an electric kettle for hot water and a box of ramen and instant oatmeal. My grandmother told me that I needed to get a job, even if it was at a fast food restaurant. I ended up working at the nearby Church's Chicken. I increasingly picked up more hours at work and started missing classes and generally losing interest in college. Eventually, I reasoned that work is more important, because what's the point of going to class if I'm not eating? That's when I dropped out of school and found an apartment a few blocks away.

In hindsight, I feel like I had been ill-prepared for adult life. I remember a meeting I'd had in high school with a guidance counselor and my mother. My grades were really good at that time, and they were trying to convince me to go to college straight out of high school. I didn't really know what I'd do, but I thought I should just work for a few years. Maybe I'd be a cook or a farmer. They hated that idea, but looking back, it would have been smarter.

I learned a few things working as a cashier at Church's Chicken in Midtown Detroit. People in that city are generally angry, especially when they are hungry and in a hurry. I also realized that white people aren't the only people that can be racist. In Redding, people called me "nigger," but in Detroit, they called me "white boy." I started noticing trends in the people that treated me badly, as opposed to the people who were friendly. It seemed like when I'd get cussed out, it was usually by black women, and whenever a white man would come in, it seemed like he'd be overly friendly. This ran counter to my previous prejudices, and it served as somewhat of an anti-prejudice, visual association exposure therapy, similar to the Implicit Association Test, where you are shown images of people and your neural responses are tested.

During this time, I made a lot of friends. There were about a dozen or so homeless people between the Church's Chicken and my apartment. When I'd work the night shift, my manager would have me throw out whatever food was left over from the day. I didn't like this very much, so instead of throwing it all away, I'd wait till he'd go into his office to count the cash and I'd open the drive-through window. All the homeless people would line up and I'd dish out the left overs for them. This became a nightly ritual and it wasn't long before they all knew me by name. Every once in a while, my manager would come out of his office and start yelling at me in a thick Bangladeshi accent, that he didn't want me giving away food, because it would just attract more of "them". Then he'd go back into his office and I'd go back to handing out the food. I didn't care much, because I knew he wouldn't fire me and I didn't like the job anyway. I hated waste, and I hated the thought of people going to bed hungry while I was throwing food away. I just couldn't do that. So, it made me feel good to do it, but another benefit was that I always felt safe walking home, late at night, in the middle of Detroit. Most of the people I passed on my walk home were the same people I'd given food to, and they'd often stop and start chatting with me about random things. One older gentleman liked to give me financial advice. One time he even stopped me in front of the college campus and proceeded to advise, in a very loud and booming voice, that I sell women's panties on eBay. He was certain I'd make a lot of money. I never did take his advice, and not just because he was homeless, more so because I never felt like selling panties on eBay was what I wanted to do with my life.

I quit my job after one year. My health issues played a role, as well as my dislike of having to be friendly to mean people, and the fact that I wasn't payed enough for it to be worth the hassle (at that time, minimum wage was $5.15 per hour and I was making $5.50 per hour). Unfortunately, things got worse once I quit my job and I increasingly became more desperate. That's when I remembered what my father had told me and I searched online for "a commune where they grow their own food." I found out that so-called "intentional communities" are all over the place, especially in America where there is a lot of religious freedom, and most of these communities are religious in nature. There's also a program called WWOOF, which stands for Willing Workers on Organic Farms. It lists farms that participate in the program and connects people who are willing to work in exchange for experience and room and board with organic farmers who need extra help. It was through this program that I found out about the Stepping Stone Farm, in Weaubleau, Missouri.

2

TORN

As it turned out, the Stepping Stone Farm was one of several communities all over the world that are owned and operated by a cult that is known as "The Twelve Tribes." They usually just call themselves "the community," and they call everything outside the community, "the world." After a couple emails and phone calls to various members of the community, I found myself at the Springfield, MO bus station, getting picked up in an old van by a long-haired, bearded guy by the name of Daveed. He had a big, creepy smile and his greyish-black hair was tied back in a fist-length ponytail. It was later revealed to me that this hair style was not only worn by all the male members of the community, but it also had historical and biblical significance. The following is a direct quote from the Twelve Tribes' website:

"Our men have beards because men were created with facial hair. It is normal and natural for a man to have a beard. Besides, it is not fitting for a priest to crop his hair or to grow long, effeminate locks. In ancient Israel both unbound hair and a shaved head were public signs of mourning or some uncleanness. It is priestly for a man to bind his hair at the back of the neck and keep it trimmed as indicated in Ezekiel 44:20: '*They shall not shave their heads nor let their hair hang loose, but they shall keep their hair trimmed.*' Priests are concerned about pleasing their Creator rather than chasing after the latest fashions."

I'd be lying if I said I wasn't a little bit nervous, leaving Springfield in this stranger's van and heading down this rural Missouri road with nothing but cow fields as far as I could see. It didn't help me feel any more settled when Daveed said, raising his eyebrows and still smiling that creepy smile, "We've made a covenant... to *die* to ourselves." Having limited experience with religion, I still didn't understand the jargon, and so when he said "die to ourselves" all I could think of was Jonestown and poisoned Kool-Aid. They didn't actually drink Kool-Aid in Jonestown (it was weakly flavored cyanide), but it has become a popular figure of speech and an infamous warning to anyone visiting a group that is suspected of being a cult: "Don't drink the Kool-Aid." I felt as if my mind was screaming, "Don't drink the Kool-Aid!" I knew what the word "covenant" meant. I thought, "I'm sure as hell not making any covenants to kill myself"!

Daveed broke the ice by talking to me about (of all things) end-times prophecy. He started off by talking about "the male child" and I had no idea what that was supposed to mean. When he said that "our goal is to raise the male child," I initially thought he was talking about he and his wife—that their goal was to raise their "male child" and I thought that was an odd way for someone to refer to their son. Then when he mentioned that it was "the male child" from the book of Revelation, I thought they believed that their son was the Messiah. Or maybe the Antichrist? I was confused, and still a little unsettled.

Of course, this man's beliefs were much deeper than I initially thought, and much deeper than I could have ever imagined. The community believed that they, collectively, were the woman from chapter 12 of the Book of Revelation:

"A great sign appeared in heaven: a woman clothed with the sun, with the moon under her feet, and on her head a crown of twelve stars; and she was pregnant and she cried out in pain as she was about to give birth. Then another sign appeared in heaven: an enormous red dragon with seven heads and ten horns and seven crowns on its heads. Its tail swept a third of the stars out of the sky and flung them to the earth. The dragon stood in front of the woman who was about to give birth, so that it might devour her child the moment he was born. She gave birth to a son, a male child, who will rule all the nations with an iron scepter. And her child was snatched up to God and to his throne. The woman fled into the wilderness to a place prepared for her by God, where she might be taken care of for 1,260 days."

The community believed that this was a figurative depiction of something that would really happen. After a few generations of "cutting off" their iniquities and being purified by the Messiah, who they called "Yahshua," they believed they would raise a pure generation, and 144,000 young men from this generation would be sent out into the world, which at that time would be extremely dangerous. The 144,000 young men, who were collectively known as "the male child," would be sent out in pairs of two to preach the gospel one final time, to anyone who would listen, before they were all killed (devoured by the beast) at the end of the three and a half years (1,260 days). The number 144,000 comes from chapter seven of the Book of Revelation. It is 12,000 young men from each of the Twelve Tribes. As soon as these young men are sent away from each community, the rest of the community will flee to the wilderness "to a place prepared for her by God." For this to happen, there would need to be 6,000 households in each tribe (two sent from each household) at that time.

The tribes were broken down into regions. The community started in Chattanooga, Tennessee, so the first tribe would have been the Southeastern region of the United States. However, every member of the community moved to Island Pond, Vermont. So, the first tribe to be named was the tribe of "Yehudah" (the Hebrew pronunciation of Judah), which represented the Northeast United States. The second community was formed in France, so France became the tribe of Reuben. The other tribes—the tribes of Gad, Asher, Naphtali,

Manasseh, Shimon, Levi, Issachar, Zebulun, Yoceph, and Benjamin—claimed Canada, Australia, Brazil, the Midwestern United States, Spain, Germany, South America, Great Britain, Central America and the west coast of the United States, and the southeastern United States, respectively. The result of Benjamin being the last tribe to be formed despite it being the birthplace of the community was that the eldest members of the community, the ones that had been there since the early 1970s, were primarily from the southeastern United States and thus became part of the tribe of Benjamin, who was the youngest of Jacob's twelve sons. Admittedly, a large portion of the world is omitted from their allotment of tribal territories, including all of Asia and Africa—the world's two largest continents—and much of Europe.

The Stepping Stone Farm was visually stunning and strikingly glorious. It was clearly well cared for, and surprisingly clean and tidy for a farm. We drove past a large, flat, grassy field. Daveed pointed out that it was their hay field and that it was fifty acres. This was the part of the farm that had been certified as organic. A line of trees, mostly pine, marked its eastern boundary, where an old railroad had been. The dirt road we were driving on marked its western and northern boundaries. As we rounded the corner and passed the line of trees, I saw an old, two-story farmhouse, very typical of midwestern farmhouses. It was white with blue trim. Then I noticed other buildings, more modern looking ones, on the property. Each one was white with blue trim. This wasn't a tradition of all the communities in The Twelve Tribes, it was just something that was unique about the Stepping Stone Farm. We passed other slightly smaller fields where livestock were grazing. We pulled into the driveway and proceeded towards a large, gravel parking lot in front of a five-acre orchard containing various fruit trees in various stages of bloom; it was late spring, 2005.

The first person I met at the farm was a tall, skinny, middle-aged black man wearing large, rubber boots. He left a few weeks later, but he still played a significant role in my experience at the Stepping Stone Farm. The man introduced himself as Joshua, but his real name was Charles Edward North III. He had a big bald spot on the front of his scalp and the little bit of hair he did have was greying. He looked down at me from thick, black, plastic-framed glasses. He had been cleaning the chicken coop, which was a daily assigned chore for everyone in the community. Mr. North's race was significant, because before I left Detroit, when I had told my father that I wanted to join the community, he had cautioned me that the Twelve Tribes were racist (based on things he had read about them online). Seeing this black man (albeit doing what many would consider to be a degrading chore) was relieving to me. *If it's safe for this man to live here*, I thought, *then it's safe for me.* In fact, there were two other people of color in that community—a woman named Naomi and her 15-year-old son, Yahalom. They both had golden-brown skin, like mine.

Everybody who was home at the time I arrived came out and greeted me with big smiles and hugs. After showing me around, they showed me to my room, which I was to share with all the single men on the farm. They called it "the single brother's room." There was a welcome basket on my bed, which I would later find out was one of the community's many traditions. It was filled with goodies and a hand-written card. I don't remember exactly what goodies were in there, but I know for sure there was no chocolate, because not eating chocolate was also one of the community's traditions. It was most likely filled with fruit, an energy bar, some sort of naturally sweetened soda, and a homemade cookie or carob brownie. They would freeze big batches of baked goods to be used for special occasions, like welcoming guests, and only took out as many pieces as they needed at one time.

The Stepping Stone Farm was a small community compared to other Twelve Tribes' communities, made up of only 12 baptized members at the time. I would be the thirteenth. The oldest members of that community were Naboth, who was originally from Colorado, and his wife, Eshet, who was originally from New Jersey. They had both joined the first community in Chattanooga, even before the community was known as "The Twelve Tribes." For a while, they'd called themselves "The Light Brigade." They didn't all have Hebrew names back then either. Naboth's real name was Michael, and Eshet's real name was Emily. The community slowly began to integrate certain traditions as they went along, like giving its members Hebrew names, celebrating the Sabbath on Saturday, the unusual hairstyle worn by its male members, and the head coverings worn by its female members during community gatherings.

The gatherings took place twice a day, morning and evening. They'd all greet each other with hugs and say "shalom." Then they would stand in a circle and someone would start a song. There was a large gathering room in the upstairs of the more modern looking building on the farm (modern looking, as opposed to the 100-year-old farm house). The walls of the gathering room were lined with banners with the names of each of the Twelve Tribes, written in both Hebrew and English. It was a spacious room, had wooden flooring, and was perfect for dancing. They did Israeli style circle dancing. The first song I heard was called "Yahshua Hears Us in the Day of Trouble" (adapted from Psalm 20). It was awe-inspiring. A thunderstorm had broken out, and a Missouri thunderstorm can be quite impressive. The thunder and lightning seemed to be keeping beat with the song. It was a simple song, just three verses, replete with minor chords and rhythmic chanting; and each line repeated once:

Yahshua hears us in the day of trouble. Yahshua hears us in the day of trouble.

The name of the god of Yacob defends us. The name of the god of

Yacob defends us.

Send us help from your sanctuary! Strengthen us from Zion! Send us help from your sanctuary! Strengthen us from Zion!

We rejoice in the name of Yahshua. We rejoice in the name of Yahshua.

And in His name, we set up our banners. In His name, we set up our banners.

We know that our God saves His anointed! We know He hears us from heaven! We know that our God saves His anointed! We know He hears us from heaven!

Some boast in chariots and some in horses. Some boast in chariots and some in horses.

But we will boast in the name of Yahshua. We will boast in the name of Yahshua.

They have bowed down and they have fallen, but we rise and stand upright! They have bowed down and they have fallen, but we rise and stand upright!

Each member was expected to share at the gatherings, which meant speaking "from the heart." It was often referred to as "an offering," and it was appropriate to give thanks, to share what you learned that day, or what you were thankful for. As a result of this teaching, members often started off by saying, "I'm thankful for…"

and then they said whatever it was they thought of to say. I always found it a bit awkward, but nothing like what happened at the end of the gathering. Each member moved closer together, forming a very tight circle. They would all lift their hands and pray out loud, looking up towards the ceiling as if to a god that everyone was supposed to be able to see, but no one actually did. They were supposed to take turns praying loudly, one after another, but occasionally, two or more members would accidentally start to pray at the same time, which could sometimes feel a little awkward.

After the gathering, we all had dinner together, and then everyone went off to do their chores. I had a dream that night: I was back in my apartment in Detroit, only most of the walls were gone, and there was no roof. I was hungry and cold, clothed in only a dirty, old sheet that was stained and torn. My landlady was banging on the door, demanding my rent money, which I knew I didn't have, and it was pouring rain; I was soaking wet. I woke up the next morning, warm and dry. I shared my dream at the gathering the next morning, and gave thanks for the warm, dry bed.

During my early days in the community, I worked in the vegetable garden alongside Ben Shimon, whom the community had assigned to be my "shepherd." I also harvested what seemed like hundreds of pounds of strawberries and milked goats twice a day with Yahalom. There was also that fifty-acre hay field. It was by far the most physically strenuous work I had ever experienced. Naboth used an old square baler to make large bales of hay, then he'd hook up his diesel pickup truck to a hay wagon and drive slowly along the rows of hay bales. All the men had to run along the trailer and toss bales up onto it, while another man would be standing on the trailer, stacking the bales. After several hours of this, I got really exhausted and thought I wouldn't be able to keep going, but then I looked up and saw Naboth's eyes staring at me through the side-view mirror of the truck, and I could just tell they were the eyes of a hard-working man that had lived a long and difficult life. It's hard to explain how it made me feel, because there was a lot to it. His eyes had a way of smiling at you, but even through the smile, they couldn't hide his sorrow. It inspired me to keep going.

Ben Shimon would often speak to me about the gospel of the kingdom—about giving up everything you have, both physical and spiritual possessions, to follow Yahshua. Yahalom, on the other hand, being a fifteen-year-old boy, liked to joke around a lot. He found some of my reactions to learning all these new things to be thoroughly entertaining. For example, I said it was kind of weird and gross, the first time I touched a goat's teats, and he thought that was hilarious. Over time, these things became normal and routine, and I also learned how to contain my reactions to everything, including physical pain and personal offenses to things I'd hear.

We had regular teachings, a few times each week, which were mandatory. Everyone would meet in the gathering room with a Bible, notebook, and pen for taking notes. They provided me with my own Bible and note-taking materials. Most of these teachings centered around the gospel of the kingdom, which Ben Shimon had already been speaking to me about every day. Sometimes, Ben Shimon would even be the one giving the teaching. At other times, it would be Naboth or Daveed. It was always taught by a man who'd been in the community for a while. So, not "Joshua," who I found out had only shown up a couple months before me, and who'd only become a baptized member of the community a few weeks before I got there. They were also not to be taught by women, although some women were designated as teachers to other women, and at times they would have a teaching for just the women, which I, being a man, did not attend, so I cannot say what was taught during those teachings. I can only guess that the women's teachings were mostly about being submissive.

I learned a lot about the Bible during the community's teachings, and I was also encouraged to read the Bible during the hour before each gathering, which was called "preparation hour." A shofar (ram's horn with a drilled-out hole for making a loud sound when blown into) would be blown three times to signal the beginning of preparation hour, so that we knew when to come in from the fields, take a shower (I would later learn that for single men, the shower was to be preceded by masturbation as needed), prayer (usually done alone or with immediate family, and while taking a walk), and then finally, reading the Bible or teaching notes (or both) to finish up the hour. At the end of preparation hour, the shofar would be blown twice to signal the beginning of the gathering.

To this day, I can tell you, without even opening a Bible, all about Acts 2:44-45 and 4:32, and how it relates to Philippians 2:4 and Matthew 6:25. The community taught that because of Yahshua's sacrifice, they have been empowered by the Holy Spirit to live together and share all things in common like in Acts 2:44-45.

"Now all who believed were together, and had all things in common, and sold their possessions and goods, and divided them among all, as anyone had need."

"Now the multitude of those who believed were of one heart and one soul; neither did anyone say that any of the things he possessed was his own, but they had all things in common."

This enabled them to obey Philippians 2:4, as it was originally written (translated from the original Greek into English, of course):

"Let each of you look out not for his own interests, but for the interests of others."

The community taught that this verse, Philippians 2:4, was tampered with by the translators of many modern bibles and that the words "merely" or "only" were added to the first part of the verse, and the word "also" was added to the second part, so that it reads more like this in many translations:

"Let each of you look out not <u>only</u> for his own interests, but <u>also</u> for the interests of others."

In fact, many translations hyphenate the words "only" (or "merely") and "also" to denote that these words have been added. The community believed that the reason the translators added these words to the Bible was because it did not make sense to the translators any other way, based on how they were living. In any society other than a common pot community, it would not be possible to not look out for your own interests, but only for the interests of others. You'd starve! Which brings us to Matthew 6:25.

"Therefore I say to you, do not worry about your life, what you will eat or what you will drink; nor about your body, what you will put on. Is not life more than food and the body more than clothing?"

In the community, the Twelve Tribes would argue, is the only place where you can truly obey these verses, because in the community, one can truly not worry about what to eat, drink, or wear, because in the community, someone else (someone who is also not worrying about these things or looking out for their own interests) will provide you with food, drink, and clothing. In this way, each member could go about doing the tasks they were given to do, not for their own gain, but for the good of the community, and for the sake of building God's kingdom on Earth.

After being taught these things, and seeing how the community lived and interacted with each other, as well as how they interacted with neighboring communities, I thought to myself, *What if the whole world lived like this? What would that be like? I want to find out!* So, from that time on I devoted myself, for what I thought would be the rest of my life, to giving everything I had, the strength of my youth, to building this "kingdom on Earth". Admittedly, I still had no understanding of the "God" part when they would speak about "God's kingdom on Earth." Nevertheless, I was baptized in the waters of Pomme de Terre Lake. I was told to "cry out" in a loud voice, for Yahshua to save me and forgive me of my sins, and so I did. I think it was Naboth, who was on one side of me, and Ben Shimon on the other. After I cried out, they lowered me backwards into the water, until I was completely immersed in the warm, shallow water. This was to symbolize being completely immersed in the community's culture, "the body" of Yahshua. Yes, they believe that the communities, collectively represent the body of Yahshua. They also believed that the communities represented the bride of Yahshua, the woman from Revelation who gives birth to the male child.

After my baptism, the nearby community in Warsaw, Missouri was notified. They planned a "First Day festival," which was a festival celebrated on Sunday, the first day of the week, by the neighboring communities. This tradition existed for all the tribes, and they usually established communities in close proximity to one another. One community was to be a farming community, which would produce food for itself and the neighboring communities. Others were to be city communities, which operated cafés that served as a means to show hospitality to outsiders, preach the gospel to those who seemed "drawn," and of course, as a last priority, to make money, which benefited not only themselves, but also the farming communities. It was a symbiotic relationship. The community in Warsaw was like the "city" community in Missouri. They currently operate a café called The Common Ground Café, but they might change the name, because there was talk about all the cafés going back to the original Yellow Deli name. The first café in Chattanooga was known as "The Yellow Deli," and more were opened up throughout Tennessee and Northern Georgia back in the '70s. They were closed down when the whole community moved up to Vermont.

Before the First Day festival, a bull was slaughtered. It was roasted on an open-pit grill on the day of the festival. Everyone from both communities feasted together; there was a teaching, and then afterwards singing and dancing. During the festival, the leaders of the Warsaw community spoke with the leaders of the Weaubleau community and I was invited to spend the following weekend at the community in Warsaw.

The main industry in that community at the time was their woodworking shop. I don't think they were even in the process of building their café yet. I showed up on a Friday, during the normal working hours and I helped out at the shop. Then that evening, we celebrated the beginning of the Sabbath. This was the tradition in all the communities. On Friday nights, there would be a large meal after the gathering, then we'd gather again to dance to Israeli folk music, and afterwards there would be dessert. On Saturday morning, there would be a sit-down gathering, which was referred to as a "double portion," because everybody was supposed to bring back what they learned that week, in addition to the usual giving of thanks. After that gathering, every Sabbath morning, there was a tradition of eating cake and yogurt. It wasn't an overly sweet cake, like a birthday cake. It was more of a somewhat dense cake, given that whole wheat flour was required, and would commonly have spices, like cardamom.

After breakfast, Eved, one of the other "single brothers," as we were called, invited me out on a canoe with him. That was a mostly pleasant experience, talking one-to-one with this new comrade of mine, this "brother" of mine, while canoeing along the Lake of the Ozarks. But then Eved and I paddled into this cove where people were diving off a tall cliff, and some of those people were women, who were wearing bikinis. I had been in the community for almost a month, and I'd had little difficulty with my status as a "single brother." No, it wasn't easy having the constant reminder of your relationship status every time someone would refer to you as a "single brother," but being away from "the world" for almost a month and not having that visual stimulation of scantily clad women, as well as being given the distraction of building the kingdom, had caused me to temporarily forget about my sexuality. It all came roaring back now, after seeing these women, and I had a difficult time over the next few days. It wasn't something I had any experience talking to someone else about, and this was before being given the "single brother's teaching."

Sometime after being back at the farm, Ben Shimon did give me the "single brother's teaching," which was like a sex talk for grown men. I had gotten offended at first, when he said that they encouraged all the single men to masturbate as needed (usually about every other day or every few days). It's something you're to do privately, in the bathroom, and you're supposed to try not to think about anything as you're doing it. It's to be a "mechanical release," and you just ejaculate into the toilet (or into a tissue and flush it) and take a shower immediately afterwards. It was difficult to hear, because it was never something I could have equated with religion before. It seemed incompatible with religion, and my experience in the community was the most religious experience I'd had. I also found it to be kind of gross and shameful, and I'd wished I could just be with a woman instead. Why couldn't I just find a wife? How long was I expected to keep doing this shameful thing? It just opened up a whole can of worms for me, and it would become my main struggle for my remaining years in the community—this thing of having to acknowledge my own sexuality for just one brief "thoughtless" moment, just long enough to have a "mechanical release" and then to have to spend the rest of my time acting as if my sexuality didn't exist.

I'd thought of these people like prophets, so I couldn't imagine that they'd teach men to masturbate, or that this was something that my shepherd, Ben Shimon, whom I'd grown to esteem as my connection to God, would do. Did the savior do this? Did Yahshua masturbate? They believed that, yes, He did. He was a man, just like any other man, who had the ability to carry the Holy Spirit within Him, like a vessel. He lived and died as a man, with divinity within Him, and He was tempted like a man, but never sinned. There are many Christians who believe that masturbation is a sin, but the community did not, at least not for single men. For the "single brothers" it was required.

Yahshua was perfect, but even so, the community would say, "Yahshua is not complete without His bride. He's on His throne in heaven, waiting for His bride to become purified, so that she can join Him." This was the theme of all their weddings. When they had a wedding, they literally put on a show. They called it a "pre-enactment." It was an enactment of events to come. The first community wedding I went to was in Manitou Springs, Colorado. I drove out there, along with Ben Shimon, Yahalom, and his mother, Naomi. It was a lavish affair. My first impression was somewhat of a sneak-peek, the night before the wedding.

All authorized weddings in the community took place on the Sabbath, so it was a Friday night when we arrived, and the band was setting up at Soda Springs Park, in Manitou Springs, right next to the community's café. The music in the community was spectacular. This was largely due to the tradition that every child raised in the community was taught to play an instrument. The children who were born there and are now in their twenties, thirties, or even forties, were quite talented after daily practice for the vast majority of their lives. There were also many talented artists who joined the community as adults. The community did seem to have a way of attracting artistically minded individuals. I was awe-inspired, once again, when the band started practicing their playlist. One song that was played at every wedding was called "Every Knee Will Bow":

The wrath of God has come, on all His enemies. Yahshua, Messiah, has won the Victory!

Every knee will bow, and every tongue confess, Yashua, Messiah, you're the King of all the Earth!

Since the entire wedding was basically just a depiction of the end of the world, "the war dance," as they called it, was a depiction of the bride (the Twelve Tribes) putting all her enemies under her feet. The dance started off with all the community members joining hands and encircling a globe, made from paper and hanging from a rotating, horizontal wheel. The groom, who represented Yahshua, tore down the paper surrounding the globe, to reveal dark banners hanging from the wheel. The paper being torn symbolized the façade of the world, which was masking the darkness within. One word was written on each banner—words like, "Pride," "Selfishness," "Greed," "Envy," and "Lust." These words symbolized all the enemies the bride must overcome to become purified. Once she overcame these enemies, she would be like the woman in Revelation 12, "with the moon under her feet." The moon is said to symbolize our bad feelings, or whatever holds us back from overcoming.

Every apocalyptic scene was played out—from the bride fleeing to the wilderness, the male child being slaughtered, and then finally, the king calling for his bride, as she ran up a ramp, onto the stage, symbolizing being called up to the sky when Yahshua returns. They would say their vows, which always involved the bride pledging to be submissive to the king, and the king pledging to protect the bride. The vows were, of course, sealed with a kiss, and then, after being joined together, the king and the bride lead the entire community in the victory dance. The guests watching everything from the sidelines, until after the victory dance when they were invited to "the marriage supper of the lamb." These weddings were not exclusive events. Outsiders were often invited, even those who were not related to the bride or groom. I can only imagine what those outsiders thought. What impression did they get, having not heard these things before? I'd heard this stuff every day in all the gatherings and teachings, but when someone who doesn't have much knowledge of the Bible or the community's teachings, accepts an invitation to one of these weddings, I can only imagine their shock!

Weddings are an emotional event for everybody involved. For this reason, there is some genuine passion in the acting-out of all these scenes. Many outsiders have become "convicted" after watching one of these weddings, and have decided to join the community. I'm not exactly sure what all the emotions were that I was experiencing at the time, but I don't think it was what I'd call "conviction." I do know there was some self-pity in there somewhere. Also, the elevation of Manitou Springs was fairly high, which wasn't good for my condition, and it was a particularly active weekend for me. I was running around a lot that day. Every member of the community was expected to help in some way. I had helped with setting up a stage, making and serving beverages for the hundreds of guests that were there, and of course, cleaning up after the wedding. So, that night, I ended up having another sickle cell crisis. This time, I was able to recover without having to go to the hospital.

I had stayed the night in a very large house—even bigger than the house I'd seen in Ann Arbor. However, even though it was the biggest house I'd ever seen, it was shared by about 20-30 people, so that made it seem a little smaller. I attended the morning gathering, still in a little pain. That afternoon, Ben Shimon drove us (me, Naomi, and Yahalom) to the café, where we got some lunch before heading back home. Community members did not have to pay for food, or really anything, within the community. This included the cafés that the community owned. They did, however, have to be sent. Which is to say that they couldn't just decide to go somewhere on their own. Whoever was in charge of their life at the time had to send them, and at that time, it was Ben Shimon who'd been given that distinction. So, I got to try some café food. Once again, I was thoroughly impressed! Sadly, the barbeque turkey sandwich from the community's café in Manitou Springs ended up being the highlight of that trip. After eating our lunch and saying our goodbyes, we drove back to the Stepping Stone Farm in Weaubleau, MO.

The Stepping Stone Farm at that time, had a very odd dynamic compared to the other communities in the Twelve Tribes; only, I didn't know that yet. What was odd about it was that the leaders were not very passionate. They didn't push the traditions as the leaders of other communities did. Traditions like the "double portion" gathering on Sabbath mornings, or anything having to do with people being forced to "come out of their shell." The leaders in Weaubleau were rather complacent in that way. It was a fairly quiet community in general, but I didn't have much to compare it to. The only time I spent in Colorado was the weekend of a wedding, so it would have been difficult to tell what that community was like from such limited experiences, and my Sabbath experience in Warsaw certainly wasn't enough to give me even so much as a hint to what communities in other tribes would be like.

There were three "elders" in Weaubleau, and one of them was a single brother. Single brothers, I would find out, were somewhat towards the bottom of the hierarchy in the communities. It's strange to say it that way, because they worship a man who was supposedly single, but that's how it was. People just didn't trust single brothers as much as they trusted the married ones. There was always that lingering accusation in your head that if someone was single, they must have an agenda. I looked up to Ben Shimon, but he really hadn't been there that long in comparison to other leaders. Neither had Daveed, but he, at least, was married. Naboth was married too, and as I said before, he'd been in the community since the beginning. So, Naboth was really the main leader of that community. He was the one who had the final say in everything. He also happened to be the most complacent of anyone.

Naboth's wife, Eshet, was in charge of all the sisters. There was Daveed's wife, Raquel, Yahalom's "imma" (that's how they say "mother", pronounced ee-muh), and Mithcah, who was from Texas. Then there were the brothers: Naboth and Eshet's nineteen-year-old son, Yatsa (he was always off making money for the community by doing construction jobs, so I didn't see him as often as the others), Yahalom, Ben Shimon, me, and another single man named "Heman." Heman wasn't around much, either. He had been a certified nurse and he had to pay child support, so the community had him work at a local hospital to earn the money for his child support payments. He'd work late and would often sleep over at his ex-wife's house. This was an extraordinary thing to happen in the community. I don't think that would have been approved by leaders of other communities—a single man who hadn't been baptized for very long, working by himself in "the world," and spending the night with his ex-wife.

Joshua was long-gone. He had been a rather religious man. Which is to say that everything was mystical for him. He would spend a lot of time stuck in his head, walking slowly and praying quietly to himself, which was very strange behavior for a community member. A typical community member (disciple) was not introverted. He was not lazy. He moved quickly, and with great determination. Whatever he was doing, he acted as if it was the most important thing in the world. And when he did pray, it was loudly! It was inclusive, too. The disciple didn't pray with his eyes closed, but rather, with his eyes wide open, and often while looking at his brothers, sometimes even making eye contact with them, and urging them with his eyes, to join in the prayer. Joshua had not been that way. And, as I found out, he hadn't even been given the name "Joshua." Like my father, he had named himself "Joshua" for religious reasons. This was also something that leaders of other communities would not have tolerated. One does not simply name oneself. A name must be given to you by someone who is inspired by the Holy Spirit.

Shortly after returning from the wedding, I received my Hebrew name. Ben Shimon had begun speaking in the gathering, about how we should all be "tender-hearted," yielding to our Father's will for our lives, always willing, and open to correction. He said that he noticed those characteristics in me, and so, he gave me the name "Lev Rak" (pronounced like "rock"). It means "tender-hearted."

My mother came to visit me, along with my sister. That was awkward. They'd never seen me be religious before. I knew they'd think I was brain-washed, and they did. I told them, "It's okay though, because I needed to have my brain washed. It had been filthy up in there!" Still, the stress must have gotten to me, because I had another sickle cell crisis. I was taken to the small hospital in Bolivar, Missouri, where they treated me for pain and I was released the next day. As it would happen, me being taking to the hospital was the best thing that could have happened to calm my mother's nerves. She later told us that her main concern was that the community would deny me of medical assistance and that they'd just pray for me instead. Seeing them do both - praying for me and providing for medical treatment, helped her to see that I was in a safe place, where people loved me. My mother and sister had left, confident that I was being well-cared for.

Not long after that, I had yet another crisis. This one was exceptionally painful. It started in my chest and soon it had moved to my whole body. I remember writhing on the floor uncontrollably. It was usually a mind-over-matter thing for me. I could make myself be calm and take deep breathes. I'd lay perfectly still and focus all my mental energy on that familiar, constricting pain. I could feel the rhythm of my heart pulsating throughout my entire body, pushing against my capillaries; this immense pressure came with each beat, making each capillary feel as if it would burst. At the same time as this pulsating, constricting pain that would come in waves, there was also a more constant, burning pain, making my blood feel like poison in my body that just needed to be removed. I could usually focus and deal with it, but not this time. Daveed had put me in a warm bath. Sometimes that helps, but it didn't this time. Finally, the brothers decided I should go to the hospital again.

Before we left for the hospital, Daveed had asked me if there were any sins I needed to confess. I searched within myself to the best of my ability. I sincerely tried to find the sins that our "abba," our

Father, was disciplining me for, but for some reason, the only thing that came to my mind was this time I'd had a particularly vivid dream and I woke up wet. It wasn't just like a "wet dream," but I'd actually wet the bed, with urine. I had been sleeping on the top bunk, and Joshua was on the bottom, so I'd really hoped none of my pee had dripped down onto him. I had gotten up and tried to clean it all up as quickly and quietly as I could. I didn't tell anyone what had happened, because I was too embarrassed, but normally I confessed everything. I didn't keep anything hidden, so that's why I'd felt guilty about this bed-wetting. The brothers forgave me and prayed for me, and then they took me to the hospital.

I spent a little more than a week hospitalized. The small local hospital in Bolivar didn't know much about sickle cell, so they sent me to a hospital in Springfield, where they also had little experience dealing with such an intense case as mine. The hospital in Springfield sent me to the hospital in Columbia, MO.

At the University of Missouri Hospital, in Columbia, it was explained to me, in no uncertain terms, that I was going to become increasingly debilitated if they did not perform a blood dialysis on me. Ben Shimon had been with me the entire time. I'd grown accustomed to turning to him for advice, but he told me that I had to make the choice this time. He couldn't decide this for me. The doctor explained to me that the sickling was centered around my lungs and that I was rapidly losing lung tissue. She said that a lot of tissue had already died. She was a persuasive woman. She was Arabic, and was wearing a hijab—not that it made her any more persuasive, but it was just something I noticed. She had told me that if I did not accept this treatment, I'd never be able to run again, that I would have trouble breathing every time I walked up stairs, and eventually I wouldn't be able to walk without having to stop and catch my breath, and I would continue to get worse until finally, I would not be able to stand up again, and I would be bedridden for the rest of my short life. "If you do accept this treatment," she had said, "you might live to be forty, and forty's old for sickle cell." Of course, I opted for the treatment. They gave me Benadryl. I'd already been receiving regular doses of morphine, but for some reason, the Benadryl had a strong effect on me. I got really loopy and decided to introduce Ben Shimon to the doctor, nurses, and all the interns. "This is Ben Shimon," I'd said, with particular emphasis on the "Ben" part. "His name means, 'son who hears.' He hears from our Father!"

The doctor had taken two 18-inch-long, flexible plastic pipelines and stuck them into two blood vessels in my leg. One was for an artery and the other was for a vein. The entry point was in my inner thigh, uncomfortably close to my scrotum. The pipelines had been connected to this washer machine-looking thing. My blood was syphoned out through one pipeline, swished around in this machine, and then went right back in my leg through the other pipeline. This went on for what seemed like hours, my balls just hanging out there for all the interns to see. It kept feeling like I was wetting myself, as this liquid was trickling out and back in again, right next to my crotch.

After returning home to the farm, I had to be confined to my bed for a while. One day, I could hear yelling, coming from down-stairs. It was something I hadn't heard since joining the community. After listening closely to the muffled, yelling sounds, I recognized the voices as belonging to Mithcah and Eshet. Not long after that, I was back on my feet, and I heard that Mithcah was leaving. I remember seeing Heman, that single brother who worked part-time as a nurse, rebuking Mithcah. "You're breaking your covenant with us!" he'd said. Apparently, leaving the community after you'd been baptized was a hurtful thing to do.

It wasn't long after that, I'd had another vivid dream. It was a sex dream: Heman was with his ex-wife. I could see her so clearly. She was tall and thin, had sandy-blond hair, and large breasts. Heman was on top of her and they were having sex, but he was yelling. "No! I don't want to do it!" he yelled, and he started weeping. "I don't want to do it! I don't want to do it!" He'd just been repeating that he didn't want to, while he was having sex with her. The next time I saw Heman, he had cut his hair. His car was loaded with all his stuff. He said good-bye to Naboth, and he was gone. I saw a lot of people come and go over the years—even people that had gotten angry at others for leaving the community.

Yahalom's imma, Naomi, had left as well—without Yahalom. She had left her son in the care of Naboth and Eshet. For a while, in the weeks leading up to his mother's departure, Yahalom had been having these laughing fits. Something I'd said had been exceptionally funny to him. Apparently, I still talked like I was from Detroit. This one night, as I reluctantly walked into the single brother's room. I loudly expressed my discontent. I looked right at Yahalom, threw my arms down at my sides in defeat, hunched my back and exclaimed, "I knew, I just knew it was going to smell like gas in here! And sure enough," I'd said, "it smells like gas!" It was a legitimate, sincere complaint, but Yahalom had thought it was the funniest thing, with my "Detroit accent" and so, for several weeks, he'd laughed himself to sleep—until the night his imma left. Then he cried himself to sleep, every night, for several weeks.

Naomi had a twin sister in the Warsaw community, whose name was Talmida. She had been married and had three younger children. Talmida had left too, and she'd left her three children with their father, Elkanah. I didn't understand what these women were thinking, and at the time I'd thought they were evil, and that's why they would leave the community and abandon their children. I don't feel that way anymore. Now I understand that people are more complicated than just vessels, containers for holding either good or evil. Now I realize that I couldn't possibly understand the pain these women must have been experiencing at the time. Everybody wants to be free, and both of those women must have felt oppressed. In Naomi's case, Yahalom wouldn't have gone with her. She offered, but he refused, and there wasn't much she could do about that. In Talmida's case, I don't think the community would have let her take her children with her, but she did eventually come back for them and she won custody of the two younger children.

Even though so many people had left, the community ended up growing significantly in my second year there. Elkanah was sent to live on the farm, along with his three young sons. Kashuv was the oldest son. He was about seven or eight. He was tall, skinny, and had blond hair, like his father, but he also had tan skin. The younger two looked just like their mother—chubby and darker-skinned. Then there was a woman from Texas, named Sharon, who came with her four-year-old son, Noah. She was baptized after about one week of being in the community. Around the same time Sharon had shown up, there was a family of four that came to visit us from Illinois— Mark, Jennifer, and their two children, Allison and Ian.

Mark and Jennifer were a typical Midwestern couple. Mark had been a manager at a dollar store. He had kind of a dry sense of humor, was middle-aged, greying and balding. Jennifer looked Romanian to me. She was skinny and had jet-black hair. Their two children looked a lot like their mother, and not much like their father. The children did not seem happy to be there. My first impression of them was that they were whiny and spoiled. I thought Ian was a dweeby, little twelve-year-old and Allison seemed like a snobby teenager who was exceptionally rude to her mother, especially compared to the community kids.

With all these new people coming to the farm, I got my first opportunities to "preach the gospel." I got a little over-zealous in my early days. I basically interrogated Ian. I asked him what he wanted to be when he grew up and he said that he wanted to be an archeologist. I asked him why and he said because he thought it'd be cool. So, I said, "But what's the point?" I kept going with that line of questioning, trying to make a point about eternity and the purpose for life. Mark did not like the way I was talking to his son and after an argument ensued, Ben Shimon told me I needed to chill the fuck out (but not in those words).

The family moved in after several visits, and Mark and Jennifer did end up getting baptized. Eventually, they received the names "Reshef" and "Amanah."

Allison was a beautiful girl. She was only a teenager, but was already more "developed" than her mother. Naturally, she and Yahalom, being teenagers, ended up getting into trouble. Apparently, they had written love notes to each other, which was a very bad thing to do in the community. The community's reaction to the situation, was what I would have expected if he'd have gotten her pregnant, or if they'd been caught with crack cocaine. They berated both of these teenagers in a meeting for several hours, and the two were not to speak to each other again. There was much stronger judgment handed down to Yahalom, because he'd been there longer and so should have known better. The rebuke continued outside of the meeting and they were both essentially shunned by the entire community and shamed for their behavior for many days afterward. It was a very public rebuke, which can be devastating to someone whose entire world is within the community, as was the case for Yahalom. He'd grown up there and had no life in the outside world—social, or otherwise.

When someone was tempted or when they went through difficult times, the community taught that they were being tested by God. It was not uncommon to witness community members shouting, "Thank you, Abba!" when an unfortunate circumstance occured. This was what community members were taught to do—to thank God when they were being tested and to pray when they were being tempted.

Like Yahalom, I had also been struggling with having these sexual urges, but not being able to do anything about it. The community acknowledged that sexuality (at least heterosexuality) is natural, but if you were single, you were supposed to act as if you did not have those desires. Such depriving of one's natural feelings can be enough to drive a person crazy. There was a woman who came to visit for a weekend. She was Greek and had a thick accent. She wore loose, gypsy-style clothing, had a beautiful, soft face, and wide hips. She was curvy and big-breasted, and was also a really good dancer. It was hard not to notice her as she danced in the circle during the Friday night celebration. Guests were encouraged to dance to the Israeli folk dances with us on Friday nights. I did my best not to stare, but she was swinging her hips back and forth and dancing way more seductively than any of the "sisters" would have danced, and at one point, I looked over at Yatsa, Naboth and Eshet's nineteen-year-old son, who was playing the guitar and he gave me a subtle nod and a knowing smile. He'd apparently noticed her too.

The thing that really did me in, was the next day, before she'd left, the woman told me that she had been in another community called "East Wind," which was a nudist community, located in the town of Mexico, Missouri. It was something to think about. I didn't know if she was heading back there or not, but I thought about her and that community for the next week. The thought of such a beautiful and seductive woman walking around naked was not an easy thought to resist, no matter how spiritual I tried to be. The next Friday night, after the celebration, and after everyone fell asleep, I packed a backpack and snuck out of the single brother's room.

I ran across the pasture and through the old railroad that had been overgrown and was lined with trees. I ran south along the railroad, towards the town of Weaubleau. Then I made my way to Highway 54 and started heading east, towards Mexico, MO. I walked about twenty miles in the dark, into the wee hours of the morning, in rural Missouri. As I walked, I sang songs from the community. One of them was another song that was always sung at weddings:

"If I could have all the riches of this world, If I could be what I ever dreamed to be.

If I could be who this world would acknowledge, my heart would not be satisfied.

Take the riches of this world away! Take the fantasies of life!

All these things have no meaning to me,

But there is something of great value, to me:

To belong to you, and to know your heart, is a treasure, above all others!

A love that will not die,

It will not pass away! It will not pass away!"

No, I wasn't thinking about some random woman I didn't know when I was singing that song. I was thinking about whoever I thought Yahshua was—whatever He meant to me. When I'd been baptized, it was on the premise of how I thought the community would change the world. I'd thought about the homeless people in Detroit—about how they didn't have much of an option to escape that life. There were homeless shelters, but they were all filthy places and one had to always be watching out for thieves. At least in the community, it was clean and filled with trustworthy people. I wanted to find out what would happen if the whole world lived like the community. There wouldn't be any poor people anymore. And it wouldn't be like just going to some charitable organization and getting a hand-out. People would actually be put to work. They'd be useful and filled with a sense of purpose. I also thought about how Yahshua had sacrificed Himself for us, so that we could sacrifice our lives for our brothers. Those were my thoughts when I'd been baptized, and that's what I'd thought about while walking down that empty highway that night. I was torn between my desire to keep my covenant and my desire to be with a woman. Both seemed equally potent.

I'd made it to the town of Hermitage by sunrise, and I went and sat in the town square. After sitting there for a couple hours, resting my feet, I got back up again and started hitchhiking. Now that it was daytime, there was quite a bit of traffic on the highway. An old man in a Buick stopped for me. He was a retired Navy veteran. I don't remember all that was said, but I do know that I'd told him about the community and that I was trying to get to a different community in Mexico, MO. I gave him a "freepaper," which was a publication that community members handed out to outsiders, much like Jehovah's

Witnesses with their "Watchtower" papers. Ben Shimon had taught me to always take freepapers everywhere I went. Although, I'm pretty sure he didn't mean that I should hand them out while I was trying to escape the community.

The Navy vet had only been able to drive me a couple miles before his turn came up. Not long after I got out of the car, a Sheriff Deputy pulled up. He asked me where I was headed and ran my license, which was from Michigan, but was still valid. After his scan came back clean, he offered to give me a ride to the county line. He said he'd radio ahead to the Sheriffs in the next county and that they could take me to my destination. So, I got in the car with him and that's when I saw Mark and Jennifer's car. It was a sporty, little Hyundai Sonata. It kicked up a bunch of dust as the driver, slamming on the breaks, veered off the highway and pealed-out, right in front of the officer. The car had come to a stop about 15 feet in front of us. Naboth, whose real name was Michael, got out of the car. The Sheriff's Deputy looked up in shock and said, "What the hell?" Then he looked over at me and said, "Wait here." I watched as Naboth pointed at me and he and the officer exchanged a few words. Then the officer walked back over to me and said, "Would you like to come with me, or do you want to go with Michael there?" I looked up at Naboth, right into those smiling, sorrow-filled eyes, and I thought about how much it would hurt him if I left. I knew he'd drove all this way to find me and bring me back, and I knew it was hurtful to everyone in the community when someone leaves. "I'll go with him," I said. "Alright," the deputy said, in a somewhat questioning tone. "You're an adult, you can do what you want." I got the sense that he was implying that I shouldn't feel obligated to stay in a cult, but that legally, I could, if that was really what I wanted to do. But was it really what I wanted to do, or was I just brainwashed?

3

A BLOSSOMING MYRTLE TREE

Naboth drove me back home to the farm. He told me he'd been going ninety miles per hour, that he'd have tried driving in every direction to find me and bring me back. It was Sabbath morning, and the community was still having their Sabbath morning gathering when we walked in. Many of the brothers and sisters expressed their gratitude that I'd made it back safely. I apologized, but admittedly it wasn't a very humble apology and I mentioned having given someone a free-paper. I talked about the decision to either go with the Sheriff's Deputy or come back home with Naboth and I felt like I'd made the right decision. Afterwards, Yatsa confronted me and reminded me about how serious it was to leave the community. If one were to leave and die out there, in the world, they would be doomed to spend eternity in the lake of fire. He reminded me about how hurtful it was to the remaining members of the community when someone they loved and made a covenant with decides to leave. Yatsa ended up leaving not long after that.

I spent most of that day in a meeting with Naboth, Daveed, and Ben Shimon. I'd confessed everything to them—the whole reason I left, and each man offered me their spiritual advice, as well as judgment as to which evil spirits were controlling me. At one point in the meeting, Naboth told me that sex is overrated. That's the one statement I remember the clearest from that meeting. After the meeting, they told me to take a walk and pray. It was clear that in order for me to stay in the community, I had to give up all of my "fleshly desires." I was still very much conflicted, so I wanted to know for sure that this was the place God wanted me to stay. I asked him for a sign. I used to enjoy watching the rabbits run around the farm as I'd walk and pray. They'd dart out of the woods and onto the path and then dart back into the woods. I didn't always see them though. So, when I did see them, it was just one of those little things in life that made me happy. So, I chose that as my sign. I said, "Abba, if this is where you want me to stay, please show me a sign. Please cause a rabbit to cross my path." Just then, a rabbit darted out in front of me and went right back into the woods. Looking back, I should have prayed for a slightly more convincing sign, like an angel or a dragon, or at least a bald eagle—something a little rarer than a rabbit.

Nonetheless, the sign had convinced me at the time, and I excitedly told Ben Shimon about it. He'd told me that I shouldn't ask our Father for a sign, and that I should believe without seeing. He quoted Luke 4:12, which is itself a quote from Deuteronomy 6:16:

"You shall not put the Lord your God to the test."

He also quoted John 20:29:

"Yahshua said to him, 'Because you have seen Me, have you be-lieved? Blessed are they who did not see, and yet believed.'"

That night, I was prohibited from joining the breaking of bread, which took place each Sabbath evening, after the resurrection cele-bration, between the baptized members who were not cut-off. The breaking of bread was referred to as "the Holy of Holies". A room was prepared with tapestries and cushions. Every baptized member who was considered to be "connected to the vine," that is to say, in unity with the rest of the community, and in communion with the Holy Spirit, shares a single, flat, round loaf of bread and a bowl of soup. They called it "humble soup" because it was to be made with just some broth and a few vegetables, so as to not take away from the main focal point of the meal, which was the loaf. Everything in the loaf represented something spiritually, and as with other symbolic representations, the community made it about them. The flour in the loaf was carefully measured out to represent each member in the com-munity. It was two-thirds of a cup for each member. The olive oil in the loaf represented the anointing, which represented the teachings that were handed down to us by God. The water symbolized the Holy Spirit, and the salt was like the correction that we receive. Then there was the heat. Heat was counted as an ingredient in the loaf, as it symbolized being purified by fire, which was all the testing and tribulation we experienced within the context of the community. After they shared the loaf, which represented the body of Messiah, a cup of wine was lifted up and blessed by two brothers or sisters, who are also considered priests (every baptized member of the community was considered to be a priest, so whichever two "have it on their hearts" to lift the cup were to step forward and do so at the right moment). The wine represented the blood of Yahshua. This was the community's version of the communion meal that other denominations of Christianity observe in various ways.

The next day, I made a more formal apology to the whole community and I was washed and forgiven. Being washed was like being re-baptized. A baptized member who had been cut-off from fellowship to the extent that they were required to miss the breaking of bread, had to be washed in order to be re-connected again. So, I went down to the water once more, and cried-out for forgiveness. Although I'd made my choice and my future seemed clear, I still struggled with the same issues.

The leaders had decided to purchase a small house along with a plot of land that was adjacent to the farm's already existing property. The property was being foreclosed on, because a meth lab had been discovered within the garage, so the community was able to obtain it at a cheap price. We were discussing names for the house, so that we wouldn't keep referring to it as "the meth house." We felt like that wouldn't "be a light to the nations," which was community jargon for how we represented ourselves to the outside world. It just wasn't going to leave a good impression to outsiders if we kept referring to this place as "the meth house." Someone suggested we call it "the Beth house" instead, because Beth is a Hebrew name. Someone else pointed out, however, that Beth is Hebrew for house, so we would have been calling it "the house house" if we named it the Beth house. Eventually, we just referred to it as "the cabin" instead, since it was so small.

The new property was filthy and cleaning it up was a tough, dirty job. The worst thing I came across while attempting to sort through all the garbage in this veritable landfill, was a chest freezer filled with plastic bags of what appeared to be human feces. After making several trips to the dump, Naboth had enough and decided to just rent a backhoe and dig a massive pit. All the garbage was thrown into the pit, the wood was burned, and metal was hauled in to the local scrap yard, which was a considerably shorter trip than driving all the way to the Springfield garbage dump. At one point, while it was just Yahalom and me—he was cleaning the inside of the house, and I was outside near the garage—I stumbled upon some old porn magazines. It immediately became clear to me that this was a test. God was allowing Satan to tempt me and He wanted to see if I'd remain loyal to

Him. It was a big struggle, which eventually ended with me praying for the strength to overcome and then tossing the magazines into the garbage pit. Afterwards I felt guilty about having looked at them longer than I should have. Then at other times, I'd wished I'd kept those magazines, like when I was attempting one of those "mechanical releases" and my mind just couldn't quite keep it mechanical.

I struggled in this way for a while, and I continued to pray to God for a wife. Then the farm in Weaubleau hosted a festival and a certain young woman came through, along with her adoptive parents. Her name was Hadassah, which, as I would later find out, is Hebrew for "myrtle tree." She was mixed, like me. She had dark, curly hair and a shapely body. She'd been a teacher for the children in the community of Vista, CA since the age of fifteen. She was now nineteen years of age. I was twenty-one. When I saw her, she was walking with a group of children, showing them the animals. Looking at her, I got this sense that was much deeper than anything I'd felt before when I'd seen an attractive young woman. This time was different. It was like a realization that God was providing me with the wife I had prayed for, and with that realization came a sinking feeling of having to be responsible. In the community, a man is responsible for his wife's soul, and married people are expected to have children. The thought of actually performing the duties of a husband and a father was a weighty thought that I hadn't yet fully entertained. Up until this point, it had been nothing but pleasant fantasies of having a Hollywood-style romance. I took a walk and prayed about it and asked God to prepare me to be a good husband and a good father. Then, after a few days, I worked up enough courage to go and speak to her father.

Hadassah's father was called Mevaser. Some had said he was the most intimidating man in the whole Twelve Tribes. As it turned out, he was the Tribal leader of Yoceph (the west coast communities of the United States). He had light, reddish hair, and it seemed his skin had the same tone. His upper teeth would rest on his lower lip in a way that seemed anything but restful. It was as if he was always about to scream, "Fuck!" Whoever he was talking to, he would look directly into their soul from piercing eyes, through perfectly round glasses that were a little too small and rested awkwardly on the tip of his nose. There was also a dignified kindness about him, a softness in those piercing eyes, and a smile on those grimacing lips. This kindness, and the respect with which he treated everybody whom he was meeting for the first time, made him more intimidating, in an odd way. It was like his character demanded your respect and adoration, and you couldn't be offended at his authority, because he was respectful and humble. So, I had approached this man and he smiled at me, and I opened-up to him, explaining the feelings I was having towards his daughter. It was a scary, vulnerable moment, but he seemed happy to talk to me.

The leaders had a meeting, and while they were in their meeting, I was asked to give a tour to Hadassah, her adoptive mother, whose name is Poriah, and all the children in their care. It was a big farm, so there was a lot to show them that they hadn't seen before, like the herd of wethered Nubian goats that we kept out in a fenced-in section of the old railroad. They kept the shrubs and bushes from becoming overgrown and they were easy to care for. I just needed to bring a bale of hay and a bucket of water to them every day. When I'd walk out there, they'd come running, with their ears flopping. It was great for the children to see. The tracks of the railroad were gone, but the gravel was still there, so it made for an easy walk, and the goats followed us the whole way. I showed them the orchard. It was about five acres and contained multiple types of apple, pear, plum, and cherry trees. I was also responsible for the care of the turkeys, which were allowed to graze in the orchard, eating grasshoppers. The whole orchard was fenced-in and the turkeys were not the greatest escape artists, so they were easy to contain. We raised 100 turkeys at a time, and I'd have to slaughter every one of them when their time came. This had been the hardest part about raising turkeys, but the meat was used to feed two communities full of people, nourishing them through the winter, so it was worth it. Sometimes, we'd even give some turkey meat to the community in Colorado. When the leaders from Colorado would come out to the farm in Missouri, we'd send them home with meat and produce.

After giving the tour to Hadassah, Poriah, and the children, we went inside the house for some tea. The leaders were still in their meeting in the gathering room, which was in the upstairs of the other building. We sat down at the dining table in the farm house, and I immediately noticed that one of the buttons on Hadassah's blouse had accidentally come undone, and I could see her cleavage. This was not something you would see every day in the community. It's amazing how many thoughts ran through my head at that moment. I think the first thought was, "Woah! That's hot!" Then I thought, "Wait, was it an accident? Is she doing this on purpose? Is her mother not going to say anything? Is her mother in on it? What is going on here?" Finally, I leaned over discreetly, while Poriah had her head turned and was talking to the children, and I motioned to Hadassah, alerting her that her button had come undone. She blushed and quickly fixed it.

There was another meeting after the leaders (elder men) had their meeting. The second meeting was called a "social meeting". A social meeting was a meeting of married couples in the community. From that point forward, I would become very anxious whenever there was a social meeting, because it was at these meetings that they decide whether or not you'll get married, or who you'll marry. For a single person hoping to get married, the social meeting had the power to decide whether they'd live happily-ever-after, or a miserable, lonely life. The single person could not attend these meetings unless the married couples already decided that they should marry someone. Then there was a betrothal meeting after a waiting period of about three months (typically).

The waiting period was a time for a young couple, hoping to get married, to spend some time together. There was to be no physical contact, just talking. Common activities among waiting period couples included taking walks, having tea breaks, or spending part of preparation time together—reading the Bible or the teachings. During this time, the married couples observed the two very closely. They watched their interactions, and they judged every word and action in order to determine whether the two were compatible or not.

After the social meeting, Hadassah and I were both told privately that we would eventually be going on a waiting period. For now, I'd be staying in Missouri, and she'd be going back to California, but I would eventually move to California. In the meantime, we were to write letters to each other. It was my responsibility to initiate the writing. I was to send a letter in an envelope addressed to Mevaser, so that it would go directly to him. He would open it and read it before giving it to her, so I was to keep it "appropriate."

After Hadassah went back to California, it became much easier for me to maintain hope, and to focus more on laying down my life, as I had decided to do. Part of my life had become a little less uncertain. I was sure of my purpose now, that I would be a husband and a father. I started spending more time with Noah, the four-year-old son of Sharon, who was a single woman from Texas. Noah became like a son to me. I taught him how to rake leaves and sweep floors, and I'd read stories to him and he'd help me do some of the farm chores. From that moment on, taking care of children would become part of my daily duties. It wasn't always easy, but it was rewarding. I felt like I was giving these children a vital foundation and it was preparing me to be a father.

Child training is an important aspect of the community, and it was one of the things that they were criticized the most for by the outside world. They have been accused of child abuse, because of their belief in spanking. To be fair, most of the accusations were over-blown. The community taught that children should be spanked on the bottom with a small wooden balloon stick when they were diso-bedient. It was a very thin, small, flexible stick, but if you hadn't ever seen it and you just heard that these children got beaten with a wooden rod, it would be very easy to misjudge the situation. They taught that the severity of the spanking should be relative to the child's age and size. A young child needed nothing more than a very light tap. It should be just enough to inflict pain, but not enough force to harm a child. The best argument against these methods involves assessing the psychological harm that a child experiences when spanked, but the accusations that the community taught parents to physically harm their children were wrong. The child training teachings specifically stated that you should never physically harm your child and you would be held accountable if you did.

Despite these teachings, there have been many documented cases of parents within the Twelve Tribes who have abused their children, and I do not discredit those who claim to have been abused personally. There have been documented cases of sexual abuse, beatings which cause bruising and welts, as well as psychological abuse. The psychological abuse is often community-sanctioned. Children in the community are not even allowed to play. They work alongside adults between training sessions (homeschooling classes). They are also spanked for the slightest of offenses, like when they say something silly, they are told they are being "foolish" and that is an offense punishable by spanking. There is even a proverb that is used to justify spanking to drive out foolishness:

Foolishness is bound in the heart of a child;

But the rod of correction shall drive it far from him. (Prov. 22:15)

Recently, the American Academy of Pediatrics released a statement: "Parents should not spank their children." Instead, they recommend rewarding positive behavior and taking away privileges or using timeouts as consequences for bad behavior. Spanking, even light spanking, has been found to cause just as much long-term psychological harm as other forms of physical abuse. So, it seems all those over-exaggerated claims of harsh beatings in the Twelve Tribes, as well as the infamous raids that have been largely ineffective, have only served to take away from what we should have been focusing on: The Twelve tribes is, in all likelihood, guilty of abusing people—both children and adults, though it is primarily psychological abuse.

Noah was the first child I had spanked. I never once did it out of anger. The teachings forbade that. The child training teachings were taught in every community, early Friday morning, before the gathering. Every adult member of the community was expected to attend, and we were to take notes. There were literally thousands of teachings centered on child training. The end goal of child training was to bring about the male child and the end of this age. The idea was that through proper child training, each generation would become more perfect than the previous generation. Each generation would overcome more of their inherited iniquities than the previous generation, until there was a generation that was completely free of iniquities. It would be from this perfect, iniquity-free generation, that the 144,000 young men who would become the male child would be chosen. For this reason, we were taught to discipline on the first command. This meant that if you gave a command to a child and they disobeyed, they were to be spanked, but out of love, not anger. You are to explain to the child, in a calm, normal tone, why they are being spanked and what they can do next time. Then, immediately after being spanked, the child was to repent, say what they were repenting for, and what they would do differently next time. Then the adult had to say "I forgive you" while giving the child a hug.

Sharon's ex-husband, Dave, came to visit for a day. I gave him the tour of the farm. Not long after that, he started calling every day. Eventually, Sharon decided she did not want to talk to him anymore. The leaders instructed the community that if someone answered the phone and it was for Sharon, to tell them she wasn't there, or that she was not available at the moment. So, Dave would call and he'd be told that Sharon wasn't available, and then he'd call right back within a few minutes. This went on for a while. I answered the phone once and he sighed and said, "Sharon, please." I said she wasn't available, and he sighed again, and with a sharp, angry voice, said, "Lev Rak! Just get her on the phone!" It was very jarring, to hear him say my name like that. I didn't even know how he'd remembered it, or how he'd recognized my voice. He was there for one day and could recognize my voice and knew my Hebrew name. At one point, Dave decided he'd drive up to the farm from Texas. He showed up right as we were having the weekly children's story. The children's stories were told on Saturday nights, after the resurrection celebration and before the breaking of bread. It had been a hot, Missouri summer evening, so we were all outside in the gravel parking lot. We had set up chairs for everyone to hear the story outside, because it was exceptionally hot and humid inside the gathering room. Dave came driving up and started doing donuts in the parking lot, kicking up gravel and sending it flying at everyone. Everybody, especially the children, were thoroughly freaked out. The leaders went and talked to him and forced him to leave. He had to drive all the way back to Texas. Eventually, Sharon did leave to be with Dave, and Noah got to be with his real father again. It was sad for me, because at the time, the community represented life to me, and the outside world represented death.

Before all this had happened with Sharon and Noah, the leaders had announced we would be opening a café in Weaubleau. Sharon got to be there for the grand opening, and she'd helped with waiting tables, but it had been a long and difficult struggle to get to that point.

Originally, the building that was to be the café had been an old bank that was built sometime in the late nineteenth century. It still had its original pressed-tin ceiling, albeit not in perfect condition. Many of the panels had large holes in them and a lot of the panels were hanging down, barely held on by a weak, rusty nail or two. Daveed had the most brilliant plan for restoring the ceiling.

The plan was so simple that it was genius. There was an old garage door in the front of the building, because after it had been a bank, it was converted to an auto repair shop. We backed one of our hay wagons in through the garage door, then set up ladders on top of the wagon. Daveed, Yahalom, and I would work one section of ceiling at a time, starting with the back of the building, which was the area that would become the kitchen. The plan was to take all the panels off from the kitchen area, and then take all the bad panels off from the front section, which was to be the dining area. We then replaced the bad panels from the dining area with the good panels from the kitchen area. Daveed had made a natural stain out of black walnut. I didn't see him make the stain, but I think he used the soft, outer shells of the black walnuts. The result was beautiful!

It had been hard work, keeping our arms lifted above our heads all day, and we had a few close-calls with the ladders slipping on the hay wagon. There was a concrete floor below us, so falling from the top of an eight-foot-tall ladder on top of a three-foot-tall hay wagon and onto the concrete floor wouldn't have ended well. After we finished restoring the ceiling, we moved on to the outside walls.

It was a brick building, and there had been quite a bit of wear-and-tear over the years, leaving large, empty holes and cracks in between the bricks. We'd set up scaffolding along the outside, and we packed mortar into the empty gaps in the bricks. It was autumn when all this work was being done, so we had to move quickly to get it done before winter.

After we finished on the outside, Yahalom and I worked together on the interior. The café meant a lot to me. I felt like I was helping to build the kingdom of God on Earth. It was also a spiritual thing for us to be restoring this old building and not only bringing it back to its former glory, but bringing it to a glorious state that this old building had never experienced before.

That winter was particularly harsh. There had been several ice storms and sub-zero temperatures. The wind would blow bitterly, and Yahalom and I were responsible for all the animals on the farm. We'd wake up early, before sunrise, bundle-up and trudge through the winter misery to take care of them. After all the farm chores were done, we'd hop into Mark and Jennifer's zippy little Hyundai and drive down to the café building. He and I worked together on the wood flooring. We screwed the floor boards onto the floor joists that Naboth had installed, and then hammered these little wooden plugs into the screw holes. Then we sanded and stained the floor. We did the same thing for the wood siding. We also installed barn wood onto the interior walls (from barns we had taken down earlier that year). We'd drive back to the farm for the evening gathering and do our chores again (Yahalom was responsible for the cows and I was caring for all the other animals). Then we'd drive right back to the café and work late into the night.

While all this work was going on, we'd listen to a lot of music. We had a few old cassette tapes that some of the communities back east had recorded. On one such tape, were the recordings of a musician by the name of Yoceph Daveed. I instantly fell in love with his music. He had an old, folk-style voice, a lot like Bob Dylan, except that he annunciated his words better. Like Dylan, Yoceph Daveed had a way of fitting in a whole bunch of lyrics into his songs in a way that still sounded nice, even though that many words all crammed together wouldn't normally work. I still remember the first time I heard one of his songs. Yahalom and I were working late at night on the café and I was tired, over-worked, and becoming hopeless, until I heard the song:

Chorus:

We can see a reflection of our maker

In all the works of His Hands

He fashioned us and made us into His likeness

That we might rule over all He made

First Verse:

From the roaring lion to the tender lamb,

Reveals the glory that is in Him

And every creature under the sun

Reveals some of who He is

From the fierce eagle to the gentle dove

He is mighty and full of love

But no one can represent Him like the creature man

Second Verse:

From a rushing river to mountain peaks

Many things in nature speak

All pointing to the one

Who created all

From the early dawn to the setting sun

We can change and be like His son,

Expressing our father's heart

When He was here on the earth

Every line in the song had been encouraging to me, reminding me of my place in God's creation, my purpose in life, and restoring my hope. Then that feeling of hope swelled up when I heard the last verse:

And in the age to come when all things are restored

The lion will lie down with the lamb

The leopard and the wolf together

We'll have war no more!

In place of the thorns a myrtle tree will grow

And the dry ground will turn into bloom

And hopefully someday soon

When He finally has our hearts...

We will see a reflection of our maker

In all the works of His Hands

He fashioned us and made us into His likeness

That we might rule over all He made

When I heard that last verse, I had shouted "Yes!" This song had given me so much hope, at a time when I was becoming tired and somewhat hopeless. It wasn't just that I'd been thinking about Hadassah a lot and her name meant myrtle tree, that was part of it, and that's the part Yahalom thought I was shouting "yes" to, so he thought that was funny, but it was also that it reminded me of what I was hoping to accomplish by laying down my life every day. All this hard work had a purpose. We were bringing about the restoration of all things! People were going to come into this café, and some of them would become disciples, that is to say, baptized members of the community, and then they would help us in building more communities, farms, and cafés, and then more disciples would come in and eventually, we'd bring about the end of the age and the beginning of the next age—the thousand years of peace.

The community taught that when Yahshua returns, there would

be 1,000 years of peace, in which the disciples of Yahshua, which included the community members, would rule over all the righteous people of the world. This was after the wicked people were destroyed in the battle of Armageddon, or Ha Megiddo. They believed that the righteous were those that have done good deeds in their life, regardless of their religious affiliation. The wicked would be those who have done evil, regardless of their religious affiliation. So, according to the community, even so-called "believers" could be wicked if they decided to do evil, and even non-believers could be righteous if they never heard the true gospel, but decided to do good anyway. Then there were the Holy, who were filled with the Holy Spirit. They were the disciples of Yahshua, who responded to the gospel by becoming nobodies in this age, but they would become the rulers in the next age. During this time of peace, the devil would be contained in a pit, but would be released one last time, to tempt those who could still be tempted. After this time of testing, the devil and his followers would be destroyed, once and for all, and the eternal age would begin. In the eternal age, each disciple would rule over their own planet, and God's love would spread throughout the whole universe. It sounds ridiculous to say now, but this is what the community taught, and what I honestly believed at the time.

We did eventually complete the café, and we received some extra help from disciples in other communities. We were trained in all the various aspects of running a café, from baking and sandwich making, to salads, wraps, and beverages. There were specific methods for doing everything, and specific recipes to follow, much like a typical restaurant chain. I was trained in the art of sandwich-making. Their sandwiches were steamed, so the meat was hot, the cheese was melty, and the bread stayed soft. The grand opening had been a huge success! People came from several miles away, because the opening of our café was the most exciting thing happening in the whole county, and it made the local papers.

During all this time, I'd been writing letters to Hadassah (by way of her father, Mevaser). I'd told her about the progress of the café and things happening on the farm, and when I'd made it through that long and arduous winter, I wrote about all the flowers blooming. It had been the most beautiful sight to me, when all the fruit trees started blossoming and all the little flowers in the vast, open fields were blooming. The winter had been replete with all forms of bad circumstances—ice storms, mass power outages, backed-up sewage. So, when springtime came, there was so much glory! So many colors! So much hope!

It had been a long wait, almost a full year, but I was eventually sent to California, as promised. Elkanah and his three boys were also sent to live out there, so we all went together in the same trip. Naboth and Eshet had driven us. My first thought, as we pulled into the driveway in Vista, was one of embarrassment. I'd written to Hadassah about flowers, and here there were flowers everywhere! There were flowers blooming all the time in Southern California! Although I'd grown up in California, I'd never been that far south, so I didn't know what to expect. It was a veritable ocean of brilliant, contrasting colors that put Missouri to shame.

Moving to the Vista community had been a culture shock to me. It shouldn't have been, because the Twelve Tribes communities boast about being in unity—one culture, shared among all the communities. My introduction to them had been in Missouri at a time when the communities there had been rather complacent. I had seen this complacency as a good thing, for the most part. I thought people should be passionate about the work they do, but maybe not so long-winded in the gatherings, not so legalistic about the teachings and traditions, and not so religious. The Vista community had kept the traditions unwaveringly. They were staunchly passionate about the teachings, and both the Southern California communities had a habit of being very long-winded at the gatherings. This commitment to the traditions was largely the result of Mevaser's leadership.

The house in Vista was enormous! I had thought those houses I'd seen in Ann Arbor and Manitou Springs were big, but the house on Foothill Drive, in Vista, was truly a mansion. However, it was being shared by about eighty people. This community was so full that it was practically bursting at the seams! It was intimidating. Although a lot of people already knew it, Mevaser announced at the gathering that Hadassah and I would be going on a waiting period. If we were seen taking walks and talking together, it was okay, because we were "covered" to do so.

There were a few reasons for Elkanah moving to California. His ex-wife, Talmida, had been living in California, and Elkanah had to meet up with her to work-out the custody issues. That's when she gained custody of the two younger children. Kashuv, the older child, stayed in the community with Elkanah. Eventually, after about a year or so, Elkanah remarried, and Kashuv had gotten not only a step mother, but also a step sister. I'm sure the time in between had been a challenge for both Elkanah and his children, but through it all, I never saw Elkanah waiver in his faith. I saw him struggle emotionally, but his faith seemed genuine and it made me respect him more.

The community in Vista decided that I should become a "training" teacher and in fact, Kashuv was one of my students. The community homeschooled their children. They called it "training." One person was appointed to be the headmaster of the school, and in the larger communities, where there were a lot of children to teach, other teachers served under the headmaster, called "Rabbi." Boys and girls were often separated into different classes to avoid distraction, and older children were often separated from younger children. This method of separating children into different classes required lots of teachers. In Vista, at the time, there were four teachers, including myself and Paul, who was the Rabbi.

Paul immediately became my role model, a greatness to aspire to. He had a certain glory about him that was not matched by anyone I'd ever met, or by anyone I've met since. If he wasn't in the community, he'd probably be described as the next Elton John, due to his incredible musical abilities, his high singing voice, and also kind of looking a little bit like Elton John. He wrote quite a few of the community's most popular songs, all of which were very dramatic and had a way of evoking powerful emotions from everyone who heard them. So, I'd known about him long before living with him. Paul's passion didn't just come out in his songwriting, he also spoke with passion, and he was very gifted at inspiring people. So, I got to work one-on-one with this man who was my role model and he taught me how to teach.

The curriculum in the community was well-rounded. They taught basic math, science, history, reading, and writing. In all of this, however, they mixed in a healthy dose of doctrine. Science class, for example, was called "creation." They did teach basic science, just like any other elementary science class, but the words "our Father" were often thrown in to emphasize that "our Father" made things the way they are. As a "creation" teacher, you might say something like, "Our

Father made water with two hydrogen atoms and one atom of oxygen." There were several history subjects and the community's textbooks on these subjects were fascinating to me. I pored through all of them. There was The History of Israel, which is taught to every child, even the very young; American and world history classes were for the older community children in America. The History of Israel was basically just Bible stories, which had been simplified and analyzed by a council of Rabbis from multiple communities, so that the moral of each story, as determined by the council, was conveyed to the children. Even their handwriting class had a strict curriculum, approved by the council. All teachings and traditions had to be approved by a council of leaders and were referred to as "the anointing." So, even the children's classes, right down to handwriting, were part of the anointing. The primary class, the most important to the community, and the first one to be taught to the children at the beginning of every school day, was called "The Three Eternal Destinies of Man."

As with teachings on other subjects that were sacred to the community, there were literally thousands of individual teachings on The Three Eternal Destinies of Man. I estimate that I taught about 500 of these teachings during my time in the community, and I read about three times as many to myself. In the Vista community, Paul taught these teachings and I would often sit in, but I would later teach them in other communities. The Three Eternal Destinies was a simple doctrine. It supposes that God created three categories of mankind: the holy, the righteous, and the filthy and unjust. The foundation of this doctrine is Revelation 22:11, but there were hundreds of other Bible verses which the community used to support their assertions on the subject.

He that is unjust, let him be unjust still: and he which is filthy, let him be filthy still:

and he that is righteous, let him be righteous still:

and he that is holy, let him be holy still. (Rev. 22:11)

The entire doctrine had been spawned by the question of what happens to the good people who never got a chance to hear the gospel. The community believed that God would judge the murderers and rapists of this world with far greater severity than the hardworking Chinese farmer who had never even heard of the Messiah, and would therefore not have had an opportunity to respond to the gospel.

Far be it from You to do such a thing as this, to slay the righteous with the wicked, so that the righteous should be as the wicked;

far be it from You! Shall not the Judge of all the earth do right? (Gen. 18:25)

This is also a doctrine that teaches, in a way, salvation based on deeds (at least salvation in the sense that one who chooses to do good deeds will not be condemned to eternal torment). This is contrary to mainstream Christian doctrine, which teaches salvation by faith alone:

For by grace you have been saved through faith; and that not of yourselves, it is the gift of God. (Eph. 2:8)

According to the community, Ephesians 2:8 was referring to the holy, that they are saved by their faith in the Messiah. The community didn't consider the people belonging to the righteous category to be saved in this sense. The holy, those who have been saved by Yahshua, would not even taste death, but the righteous would, along with the filthy and unjust. The difference between the two categories that do have to go down into death is what happens at the resurrection at the end of the next age:

The sea gave up the dead that were in it, and death and Hades gave up
the dead that were in them, and each person was judged according to what he
had done. (Revelation 20:13)

Do not be surprised at this; the time is coming when all the dead in the graves will hear His voice, and they will come out of their graves:

those who have done good will rise and live,

and those who have done evil will rise and be condemned. (John 5:28-29)

When it comes to the question of people being judged as either believers or non-believers, with non-believers being judged equally, regardless of their deeds, or whether they'll be judged individually based on their deeds, I would say that the community had the moral high ground. Of course, trying to prove one's point solely on Bible verses can be a tricky thing to attempt, and with this subject, it gets really confusing. Not only are there verses that seem to support the doctrine of salvation based on deeds and others that support the doctrine of salvation based on faith, there are also verses that seem to support both the doctrine of a deeds-based judgment *and* only two, not three destinies:

> *God will give to each person according to what he has done.*
>
> *To those who by persistence in doing good seek glory, honor, and immortality, He will give eternal life.*
>
> *But for those who are self-seeking and who reject the truth and follow evil, there will be wrath and anger.* (Romans 2:6-8)

Of course, it shouldn't come as a surprise to anyone that a collection of sixty-six different books, written by different authors, would have conflicting passages, resulting in conflicting doctrines and multiple denominations (divisions) of faith. So, that's the Three Eternal Destinies, in a nutshell, and I cannot emphasize enough how important this doctrine was to the community. They taught it to their children; they taught it to the adults. They spoke about it in their gatherings and they preached it to Christians they were hoping to convert.

As hard as it was to live with about eighty different people, as difficult as the culture shock had been, moving to a community that was so adamant about upholding the traditions, the biggest challenge for me had been living with Hadassah. We did often take walks, and I'd overhear people say things like, "Those two have *got* to get married! I mean, just look at them together!" A lot of people thought we made a good couple. They thought we *looked* good together. They said a lot of things that they shouldn't have said—at least not according to the community's guidelines for waiting periods. It had drawn on like this for a very long time. At one point, I remember walking out to the patio in the back of the house, and Hadassah had been there. The hillside behind her was filled with cactuses of various colors—orange, purple, and green. There were potted trees and flowers on either side of her. One tree, I'd been told, was a myrtle tree, and it was blossoming. Hadassah had a large hibiscus flower in her hair and she smiled at me. It hurt. I remember thinking that it was like looking at a Missouri sunset over the wide, open fields: so beautiful that it hurts, because you know you'll never be able to have it, keep it, and hold it in your arms; and just like with the sun, the more I looked at Hadassah, the more it hurt. Sometimes beauty can be incredibly cruel.

4
ABRA-CHAM

During my time in the Vista community, I'd often been sent out evangelizing. Every Wednesday, I would be sent to the Ocean Beach farmer's market, in San Diego. I would make several gallons of yerba maté, which was the community's favorite tea. There was a drink they liked to make called "common ground," which was made to taste like a fancy coffee beverage using roasted maté, peppermint, chicory, a bunch of honey, and half-and-half. So, I'd make this common ground as well as chai maté, and bring that to the market. Another brother would bring the community's "hippie bus" (that's really what they called it), which was an old, refurbished school bus that was painted to look like an old, psychedelic hippie bus. A handful of disciples from both the Morning Star Ranch and the Vista community would show up and play music in front of the bus; Paul and I would setup our booth and sell maté, hand out freepapers, and speak to people about the gospel. Every once in a while, Paul would sing one of his songs and it was beautiful!

I was busy serving tea at the booth one evening, when I heard this sharp, jarring voice, "Lev Rak!" I looked up, and without missing a beat I just said, "Dave, huh?" It was Sharon's husband, Dave. The man who'd been so intimidating to me during our brief encounter in Missouri. Here he was, almost 2,000 miles away, with a young blonde woman hanging on his arm. I knew that Sharon had left the community to be with him, so without thinking I asked, "Where's Sharon?". He said she was still in Texas and that their son, Noah was doing well, and that was pretty much the end of the conversation.

My sister was living in San Diego at that time, so she'd come to visit me frequently—either at the market or in the community. The conversations were usually friendly and casual, but on one occasion she'd asked me what I thought about gay people. My first reaction was to say, "I don't." I didn't know why she was asking me this, because homosexuality was just not something I'd normally think about. We did have an uncle who was gay, but I'd pretty much severed ties with the whole family, so my uncle's sexuality was of no concern to me. Even so, she really wanted to know what I thought about it and the answer I gave her was the community's doctrine on the subject, which is not what I currently believe. The community taught that love bears fruit. So, the love between a man and a woman is fruitful, producing offspring. This is not something that two men or two women can do, so in the community's opinion, homosexuality is not love. I've since grown to hate analogies and I now see it as an insult to an individual's intelligence to assume that they need to hear an analogy before they'll understand a concept. Analogies can only go so far, and this analogy of fruitfulness clearly falls short, because what about the love between parents and children, or between siblings? Nonetheless, I'd said it, and I'd said it as if it was my own opinion, so my sister's reaction was to get angry with me and the conversation ended with her shouting, "I just hate you so much, because I'm just so tolerant of everybody!"

It was also during this time that I was sent out "walking" for the first time. Much like the Mormons, the community sent people out walking in pairs. It was usually two men, but it could also be a married couple. Walkers were sent out with a backpack full of freepapers, one water bottle each, and occasionally a sweet, flakey granola-like thing that they call "walker's bread." It was like sweetened bird seed. They used a small, round, yellowish-white grain called millet, which is, not surprisingly, usually used as bird seed in America. They somehow made a dry, crumby, cakey cracker out of the stuff. Other than that, walkers had to depend on others' hospitality if they wanted to eat and drink anything while they were away from the community.

I had been sent out with a young man named Elahav. He and I were about the same age and had joined the community at around the same time. We walked from Vista to Oceanside, talking to people and handing out freepapers along the way. We'd actually crossed paths with a pair of Mormons once. People were mostly polite, but didn't want to be preached at. We talked to a young woman who was probably still in high school and she told me I had dreamy eyes, so we kept on moving. For some reason that I am now unsure of, we decided to stop in a Reggae music store. I happened to come across a CD from my old friend, Ras Kente, with his picture on the cover.

The rest of our walk had been largely uneventful. We'd slept on the beach that night after being shown hospitality at a local Mexican restaurant. The owner of the restaurant, I would later find out, had a history of being friendly towards the community. We'd walked back to Vista the next day, after walking all around Oceanside and Carlsbad, and we showed up at the community a little earlier than expected. Mevaser had been disappointed in us. Nobody was saved or even visited the community as a result of our walk, and we'd come home too early. It had been a long walk and we were both sore and tired, and I guess we just weren't feeling it anymore. Seeing Ras Kente's face on that CD cover had really gotten to me though. I thought a lot about the whole Rasta culture, about my dad, and about how I wished more people from that culture could come and join the community to be saved. So, I proposed an idea for a freepaper to Mevaser.

We called it, "Rasta Dreams." I had written down my story—the son of a hippie woman and a Rasta. I wrote about how hurtful it had been to grow up without a father, and I wrote about the hope I'd been given since joining the community. I also contacted a couple of other disciples who had previously been part of the Rasta culture and we put all our stories into one paper. Paul edited the paper, and Mevaser, who operated a print shop, printed-out thousands of copies. I'd been sent, along with the other disciples who'd contributed to the paper, on somewhat of a tour to various Reggae and Rasta-themed events to hand out the Rasta Dreams freepaper.

All this evangelizing had been a welcomed distraction for me. The longer the waiting period with Hadassah was drawn-out, the more anxious I'd become. I had wanted so badly to get married. I felt like getting married and having children was the one thing that would have completed me. It became harder and harder to get my mind off of it. Meanwhile, Hadassah had grown colder towards me. She used to smile warmly and softly, her eyes sparkling every time she'd see me, but now that was gone. Four months had gone by, and several social meetings. Each time there was a social meeting, I'd think that maybe that one was the one that they'd decide Hadassah and I should get betrothed. Eventually, however, they decided that there should be a break in our waiting period. They called it a "parenthesis." I was sent to live at the Morning Star Ranch for an undetermined amount of time.

At the Morning Star Ranch, all the single brothers lived in yurts.

There were more than twenty of us and we were crammed into two tiny yurts with bunk beds that were way too close to each other. After about one week at the ranch, I had another sickle cell crisis. I had some pain pills that had been prescribed to me by a doctor in Missouri, so I was taking these pills and trying to rest on a twin mattress, on a top bunk, in a crowded yurt. In the daytime, it would get way too hot and at night the temperature would plummet. At one point, I thought that I should go to the hospital and the man who'd been like the shepherd of the single brothers said that the doctors at the hospital would have nothing to offer me and that our Father knew my body better than those doctors did. He had also told me that I should stop taking my pain pills, because they did nothing to solve the problem and they merely masked the pain. I knew better at the time. I'd been told by doctors that the pain medication actually served to dilate the blood vessels, which can help the sickle cells to flow through, rather than getting stuck. Simply being relaxed can stop the chain reaction that occurs when your body tightens up from the pain, preventing the sickled cells from becoming stuck in the blood vessels. Even so, I wanted to be obedient. This brother had been in the community for almost twenty years, and as my shepherd, he was speaking from God. That was what the anointing taught. So, I stopped taking the pills and just dealt with the pain, trying to master it with my mind, trying so hard to just be obedient to God, who was speaking to me through my brothers. I got through the crisis, and I felt like it was a miraculous healing, like God Himself had healed me, even without doctors or pain medication. I was feeling encouraged for the next week after getting better, but then that same brother who'd told me to stop taking pain pills for sickle cell, ended up having a toothache, and he came to me and asked me for my pills… for his toothache.

While Hadassah and I were separated, there had been a huge wildfire. It affected both communities, and both had to be evacuated. It had been decided that the two communities would wait out the wildfire together at a campground in Lake Perris. It had been hard for me to see Hadassah again, and I still wasn't sure how she felt about me. Mevaser told us that we should spend some time together, so we took a group of children on a hike and then went swimming. Hadassah jumped in the water, but I just watched from the shore. Community girls didn't wear normal bathing suits, because supposedly, bathing suits were considered immodest. They usually wore a shirt and short pants to go swimming. So, Hadassah came out of the water, with her shirt clinging to her body, and she sat down next to me on the beach. She was shivering, and she looked over at me with that same warm smile I'd remembered, and with that familiar sparkle in her eyes. "I missed you," she said. It cut into me deep. I wanted to put my arms around her. I imagined how that would feel, and I'd thought about it so hard that I could almost feel her shivering body in my arms. "I missed you too," I said.

Both communities had narrowly missed being burned to the ground. At the Morning Star Ranch, the fire had crept up so close that it had burned the other side of the hill that was behind the property, before it had been extinguished. After the wildfires, I was sent back to Vista to continue the waiting period with Hadassah. After another four months, it had gotten to the point that we'd started having special dinners with some of the older married couples. This was the last step in the waiting period before a couple was betrothed. The waiting period couple would be interviewed during the meal and the older couple would determine compatibility. We dined with a few different couples, night after night. Some of the couples flat-out told us that we'd definitely be getting married, so I was sure of it by then. I was excited, happy, and hopeful about our future together. Hadassah and I had even talked about how many children we wanted to have. I'd said twelve, but she thought maybe not so many. The married couples invited us to their next social meeting. *This was it.* I went into that meeting completely certain that we'd be betrothed. That would have been the only reason for inviting us to a social meeting. However, Mevaser told us he was calling off the waiting period and that I'd be moving to Hiddenite.

Hiddenite is a town in North Carolina. The community had bought an old inn and banquet hall, as well as several adjacent properties with smaller houses on them. It served as the perfect complex for hosting councils with community leaders from all over the world.

It was also where Yonéq and Ha Emeq lived. Their real names were Gene and Marsha Spriggs. They were an old married couple, and the founders of The Twelve Tribes. Other leaders in Hiddenite at the time were Yohanan Abraham, who was the main mastermind behind the "Cham" teachings (Cham is pronounced with a hard, clearing-of-the-throat, 'H' sound and an 'ah'), Soreph Gamaliel, who had a PhD in chemistry from MIT, and Daveed Zarubbabel, who was a computer programmer who also had a degree in religious studies. All of these men wrote extensively for the community; they wrote the teachings, textbooks, and freepapers. Everything had to be thoroughly researched, prayed over, and brought before councils of elders. This is where the anointing came from, and this is where I'd be living.

Only a few days after the decision was made in the social meeting, I had a plane ticket in hand. I'd be travelling alone, with no money, no phone, just a plane ticket, my clothes, and a few sandwiches. I asked the brother who'd dropped me off at the airport what I should do if I missed my connection and he told me to call The Twelve Tribes' hotline. It's a toll-free phone number that is on all the freepapers. If I called the number and told them who I was and where I was going, they'd be able to contact Hiddenite and let them know. So, I hugged the brother good bye, and that was that. I was on my own. I made my connections just fine and landed safely in Charlotte. I was thrilled to find that the disciple who was waiting for me at the airport was none other than Yohanan Abraham himself.

I had struggled immensely with the Cham teaching when I'd first heard it. It was based on Gen. 9:20-25:

Then Noah began farming and planted a vineyard. He drank of the wine and became drunk, and uncovered himself inside his tent.

Ham, the father of Canaan, saw the nakedness of his father, and told his two brothers outside.

But Shem and Japheth took a garment and laid it upon both their shoulders and walked backward and covered the nakedness of their father;

and their faces were turned away, so that they did not see their father's nakedness. When Noah awoke from his wine, he knew what his youngest son had done to him. So he said,

"Cursed be Canaan;
A servant of servants
He shall be to his brothers."

He also said,

"Blessed be the Lord,
The God of Shem;
And let Canaan be his servant.
May God enlarge Japheth,
And let him dwell in the tents of Shem;
And let Canaan be his servant.

The community taught that race-based slavery exists because of this one disrespectful act of Cham against his father, Noah. Because of this one act, all descendants of Cham, which were called Canaanites in the Bible, were to be slaves to Shemites. This curse was to last for the entire age—until Yahshua returns. The Bible calls this cursed race "Canaanites", because Cham's son was named Canaan, and they are all descendants of him, but the community called this race "Chamites." Now, when the community uses the word "Chamite," they are referring specifically to black people. This distinction was based on the father's lineage, so because my father was a black man, I too was considered Chamite by the community. The community believed that all black people are somehow descendants of Canaan, that all white people are descendants of Shem, and all Asians are descended from Yapheth. They taught that all are equal in Messiah, because once an individual had been baptized into Yahshua and received the Holy Spirit, all curses would be lifted and all would become servants of God. However, they believed that in the outside world, all black people are to be servants of white people if they are to be righteous. I now believe that this notion of justifying slavery based on race is morally repugnant. There is no excuse for it, and it should have caused me to disavow the community and admit that there was no way that the Bible could be the inerrant word of God if this was what it teaches, but I wanted so badly to believe that the community was everything I'd thought it was in the beginning, and I wanted so badly to humble myself and just be obedient to God, that I accepted this teaching as truth. After all, if this was how God made it, who was I to argue?

Yohanan Abraham was an older black man with a rat-tail for a ponytail. He had joined the community in Chattanooga, way back in the very beginning. He was thin-bodied, sharp-minded, and spoke with a fiery passion. He'd often told stories about Nathan Bedford Forrest, who'd founded the Ku Klux Klan. Yohanan Abraham believed that Nathan Bedford Forrest was a righteous man, and he believed that the KKK, in its early days, had a righteous purpose. He talked about the period of time after the Civil War, when the South had been reduced to ashes and there was a time of restoration. The North sent people en-masse to the South and many of those people were black men from the northern ghettos (according to Yohanan Abraham). These black men supposedly ran wild, raping white women—and northern judges who were appointed in the South would often not convict these out-of-control black men for their crimes. So, Nathan Bedford Forrest came up with the Klan to scare black men into submission. He knew that black people were notoriously superstitious, so he and his men would put on white robes to make themselves look like ghosts. Their plan worked and order was restored in the South.

I had watched *Chappelle's Show* before joining the community.

It was one of my favorite shows. So, admittedly, the image of Chappelle's black white supremacist character was lingering in the back of my mind when I was listening to this older black man glorify Nathan Bedford Forrest and the KKK, but I would never have told anybody that. I had a lot of questions on the ride to Hiddenite, and fortunately, I had a lot of one-on-one time with Yohanan Abraham. I'd been wanting to write a paper that was specifically for black people, just as I'd written a paper for Rastas. I was excited about the idea of more black people joining the community. He told me that in general, people did not like being targeted and that ultimately, Chamites need to hear the gospel from Shemites, rather than from other Chamites. All of this had been confusing to me, because I thought all were equal in messiah, and yet, the community still taught inequality. They taught that mixed-marriages didn't work because the races are just too different. They taught young Chamite disciples to be humble and submissive to their Shemite brothers, and they quickly raised-up young Shemite disciples to be leaders. To be fair, there were many Chamite leaders in the community as well, but it took longer to become a leader if you were a Chamite. We talked about a few other things too, like the stereotype of ghetto black people and how most black people are middle-class suburbanites and wouldn't be able to relate to the whole ghetto mentality. Then Yohanan Abraham mentioned that there's another Chamite disciple living in Hiddenite. He said his name was Charles and asked if I'd heard of him.

Joshua Charles Edward North III was there to greet me, along with the few permanent residents of the Hiddenite community. Surprisingly, sharing a room with him had been a relatively pleasant experience. Our room was above the kitchen in the banquet hall. It was spacious, had big beds, and even a bathroom. The community operated a bakery business and they'd often leave leftover treats they were unable to sell on a rack in the kitchen. We were allowed to go down there whenever we got hungry to grab something from that rack. This was, of course, in addition to the regular three meals per day we'd receive, which were of particularly high quality in Hiddenite. It was by far the most comfortable place I'd stayed at in my entire time with the community.

Charles and I had a lot of catching up to do. The community wouldn't allow him to use the name Joshua, since he'd given himself that name, so they called him by his actual first name. He'd left the community in Missouri, but somehow reconnected with them in the tribe of Benjamin. He'd been the reason I'd stayed in the community in the very beginning, and now our Father had brought him here, right at the same time our Father had brought me here. Charles had shown up just a few short weeks before me, just like it had been when I first moved to Weaubleau. I knew it must have been our Father bringing us together again. The leaders had decided that I'd grow a garden and Charles was to help me, but in the meantime, since it was still early in the season, I stayed busy with planning and helping

Charles with handy work around the complex, like painting, and running errands. We also helped with the care of the goats and cows.

At one point, Charles and I were sent to Chattanooga for a week. They were building a new Yellow Deli in Chattanooga and it was one week before the opening day, which had already been announced. The deli wasn't ready yet, so it was all-hands-on-deck, with brothers from all the communities in the tribe of Benjamin working night and day to get the deli ready. I was helping with dry wall in a house the community had just bought for the purpose of housing the new deli staff. I had met Yonéq and Ha Emeq, just a few days before getting sent to Chattanooga. During this time, they'd been making frequent trips between both communities, so they weren't in Hiddenite when I'd first arrived, but they showed up about a week later.

My first impression of Yonéq was that he looked just like the classic image of Colonel Sanders. He had the white hair, southern accent, glasses, and the same friendly Colonel Sanders smile. Ha Emeq was just incredibly giddy all the time and she spoke with a high-pitched voice. She just seemed generally high on life. Ha Emeq always had a group of young women with her, which she called "The Shiners." It was kind of a play on words, because it was like the Shriners, but they were supposed to shine a light, in a spiritual sense. They served as Ha Emeq's apprentices. She passed on her wisdom to them and they constantly helped with serving, cooking, cleaning, and odd jobs around whichever communities in which Ha Emeq happened to be. While in Chattanooga, Ha Emeq made an announcement at the dinner table regarding her next round of Shiners. Sure enough, Hadassah was one of them.

My first thought was, "What are these people trying to do to me?" I didn't know whether they wanted us to be together or not, but then I resolved to the more likely scenario, which was also the humbler thought: This had nothing to do with me. This was for Hadassah's spiritual growth—nothing more, nothing less. They knew this was a difficult time for her and that she would benefit from Ha Emeq's guidance. I went back to Hiddenite and quickly got to work with my garden, attempting to push Hadassah out of my mind.

I was given everything I needed for my garden: Seeds, irrigation supplies, a rototiller; they even had a bunch of guys help with putting up a tall wooden fence for keeping out all the critters. I used the rototiller and a dirt rake to make raised beds and I got a bunch of cedar chips and sawdust from a local sawmill, which I used as mulch in the walkways. It was beautiful! A lot of people had told me it was the most beautiful garden they'd ever seen. I planted three different plots throughout the complex and the total land used amounted to more than an acre. It supplied the community with all the vegetables they needed during my time there, even enough for feeding the large coferences they were hosting. The garden had become my primary focus—

above everything else, despite the community's teaching that Yahshua should always come first. Nobody seemed to notice or care that my priorities had shifted. In fact, people praised me for it.

During all this, Charles, who was many years my senior, in regard to age, seemed to resent having to be my helper. I understood this, and I was never a harsh taskmaster, but at the same time, he'd left the community and his total amount of time spent there was only a few months. I was in my third year, so in that regard I was his senior. That's the way I saw it and that's how everyone else in the community saw it too. He'd often walk as slow as humanly possible, and he was a tall man with very long legs, so it looked ridiculous. Even Yohanan Abraham lost his temper with Charles at times, due to how obstinate the man was. It also irked me how religious Charles was. He'd pray for a good five minutes every time we'd get into a vehicle, even if we were just hauling some manure across the street! I couldn't understand how someone could be so pious and so incredibly lazy and obstinate at the same time, because normal disciples in the community were not like this. Even so, we had some good moments too.

When he wasn't being pious, Charles could be really light-hearted and he loved telling bad jokes. He gained such a reputation for his bad sense of humor that one time he said, "I have a joke," and everyone within ear-shot immediately burst out laughing. Then he told some cheesy joke about a nail talking to a hammer and no one laughed. I loved that about him. I loved it when Charles was just a normal, light-hearted person, because that's how the community's disciples were most of the time. In general, community members were just normal, humble people who weren't too religious to tell jokes. They worked hard, they prayed, and they did their best to get along. That was the thing with Charles: He didn't know how to get along. He was not a conformist. His religion had been his own, and not that of the community. Looking back, I can't blame him for that, but I did feel bad for him. Most of the time, he was as serious as a heart-attack, and he just did not seem happy to be there. Halfway through the summer, Charles got invited to go to a community wedding in Boston. He went up with a van full of disciples and when they arrived, he got out of the van, grabbed his bags, and walked straight to the bus station. He ended up going back to his own home in Oklahoma, but it wasn't the last time I'd hear from him.

For a while, the garden proved to be an effective distraction from my struggles. The largest of the three garden plots was across the street from the main compound. It was on the edge of a forest and I used to spend a lot of time imagining that I was in the wilderness and growing food for survival. I had a compost pile in a clearing in the woods. It was enriched with all the bedding from the barns and all the food scraps from the kitchen. There was a natural gateway, a pink and purple arch, leading to the compost. It had been formed by two dogwood trees with pink blossoms and an arching kudzu vine with purple blossoms. There was also a creek running through the woods, so the whole place was just peaceful and glorious. This peaceful, wilderness living was a long-held fantasy of mine and it would continue to be throughout my time in the community. My fantasies were a comforting escape, a way for me to be alone in my own little world and not have to listen to anyone. But at the same time, I was doing real work, enabling me to continue to live this other life in my head, completely undisturbed, because to the outside observer I was a hardworking disciple of Yahshua.

I lived this way for a few months while I was in Hiddenite, entirely content in my lonely, wilderness garden fantasy, until one evening, during a conference, when The Shiners showed up. Hadassah walked into the banquet hall, wearing this beautiful, dark purple dress. One look at her smiling face from across the room, her curly hair gracing her soft, round face, and I was instantly immobilized by that sharp, stabbing pain in my gut. My chest tightened up and started burning. My eyes burned too, and I went out the back door and ran across the street to that peaceful sanctuary that was my garden at the edge of the woods. I fell to my knees in the darkness and prayed. I prayed and cried, and all those suppressed emotions I thought were gone just came flooding back. It was clear to me that whatever I was doing, it wasn't working. I needed to devote myself to my spiritual growth if I was to find true inner peace and contentment.

Given that I was in the same community as some of the Twelve Tribe's most prominent leaders, I sought to learn what I could from them. Yonéq would often read teachings when there weren't conferences happening. When it was just the permanent residents of the Hiddenite community, we didn't have normal gatherings like other communities. We just had sit-down gatherings where teachings would be read. Sometimes Yonéq would read from a freepaper. Once he even read the Rasta Dreams paper to everyone. I was perplexed by this man who'd founded the Twelve Tribes. He had a teaching for everything. There were even teachings on not being wasteful. Then I'd see him excessively hosing-off the driveway. He'd do it all the time, even when it didn't seem like it needed it, and all I could think was, "so much water is being wasted!" Once, during a conference, when the banquet hall was filled with people and we were having a regular stand-up gathering, Yonéq called out this sister who was a bit on the heavy side. He was speaking about over-eating when he looked at this woman, called her by name, and said she was fat. He started talking about how she was living in sin and needed to repent for her lack of self-control. She broke down in tears and repented, but this had kind of shocked me a bit. He even called me out once. We were all eating sweet corn from the garden, and I guess he must have gotten an ear that had crossed with some more starchy corn, or maybe it was just a recessive gene that just happened to come out in the ear he got, but at either rate, he got an ear of corn that wasn't sweet. "Lev Rak!"

he'd shouted, from across the room, "how come my corn isn't sweet?" I'd been just as baffled as he was, since all the other corn tasted great. What really got me though, is this was odd behavior from someone who's always teaching people to never complain and to be thankful for what they have. I mean, it was still food. I'd worked hard to grow it and we weren't starving, so there was that to be thankful for. Of course, I would have never said that out loud. I just maintained a subservient attitude like everybody else.

Then there was Soreph Gamaliel, the genius doctor of chemistry from MIT. He was one of the community's most prominent rabbis. One time, I was in the banquet hall and it was completely empty. The whole compound was eerily empty when there wasn't a conference going on, because suddenly it would go from 50 to 100 people to just 15 to 20 people, sharing this large property with several houses on it. So, I was in the banquet hall on a Sabbath, reading the Bible, and Soreph Gamaliel came up and sat down next to me. "You know," he said. "You could marry anybody you want to." He started talking about how I had all three races in me, so it wouldn't matter who I married, because it would be a mixed marriage regardless of my wife's race. The community believed that Native Americans are descendants of Yapheth, Europeans are descendants of Shem, and Africans are descendants of Cham, so I would be all three. I'm not sure why he'd brought it up. Maybe it was to console me, because he'd been aware of my waiting period with Hadassah and how difficult it had been.

The community seemed a little obsessed with race. Even Ha Emeq, Yonéq's wife, had talked to me about my race. She said I was special, because I could relate to people of all races. They believed that each race had its own set of iniquities and that's why it was hard for people of different races to relate to each other. But if I could overcome my iniquities, I could lead others and help them to overcome in the same way.

Yohanan Abraham hosted open forums once every week. It was an opportunity for outsiders to come visit and ask questions and a chance for us to openly speak about our life, about politics, religion, virtually anything people wanted to discuss. Yohanan Abraham was a brilliant man. He spoke eight different languages. One time, while he was helping me clean the goat pen, a couple Korean women pulled into the driveway and asked for directions. Yohanan Abraham detected a Korean accent, so he gave them directions in Korean. It was priceless, seeing the shocked look on their faces, when they saw this old black man in rural North Carolina, holding a pitchfork, answer them in fluent Korean. It had been just as priceless every time the issue of race came up and he would speak about how the only hope a black person has of being saved, is to submit to a white man. Of course, when he said that, the "white man" he was referring to was Yahshua, the messiah. It was still entertaining to see the reaction on white people's faces to hear this blatant racism from a black man. You could tell they really wanted to get offended and angry, because they'd been taught their whole lives that racism is wrong. They never allowed themselves to be racist, but they were just too confused to get angry, because how could they tell a black man that what he's saying is racist against black people, when they were white? Furthermore, being a humble man that received direction every day from the white men he lived with, he was living what he preached, and how could they get angry at that?

There was one family that tended to frequent Yohanan Abraham's open forums more than anyone else. They loved listening to him, Yonéq, Zarubbabel, and Soreph Gamaliel so much that they eventually moved in. Caleb, the oldest son in this family, was just a couple of years younger than me, so they thought it'd be a good idea for him to work alongside me in the garden. It was my duty to preach the gospel to him while we were working, so I obliged. Having the sense of being responsible for someone else's soul is a great motivator for maintaining a spiritual connection with Yahshua. What that means for a disciple in the Twelve Tribes, is obeying the anointing, as well as your brothers and sisters, because Yahshua speaks to you through them. The anointing covers literally every aspect of one's life, from how you pray, how you think, and yes, even how you wipe your ass. There really is a teaching about taking three to four squares of toilet paper, folding it to the size of one square, then wipe, fold, wipe, fold, and repeat until you have this tiny, poop-stained square that you flush. This is much less wasteful than wadding up a whole bunch of toilet paper every time you wipe. So, I strove to be obedient to the anointing in every way, which includes, but is not limited to, wiping one's ass.

The gospel isn't the entire anointing, so it wasn't like I was working with this young man in the garden explaining to him how he should wipe his ass. The gospel is essentially total surrender. So, preaching the gospel is, simply put, telling your story to someone, of what made you completely surrender your life to Yahshua. The more surrendered someone is, the more powerful their message will be, hence the desire in me to be totally surrendered to the anointing so that I could lead this young man in the right direction. Caleb had asked me some tough questions, like how does a young man go about getting to know a young woman. I told him my story, which in retrospect, as hard as I'd been on myself, was a story of surrender. There had been plenty of young people who didn't have the same respect for the anointing as I did, who just gave into temptation instead of allowing their lives to be handled by others. Rather than listening to the community, letting God decide if they can get married or not, they'd sneak off and have sex. At that point, a couple is forced to either get married or leave. If they choose to stay, they are given what is referred to as a "brown pants wedding", which is a shameful, impromptu wedding in which the couple wears whatever work clothes they happen to have on instead of white robes. It is more of an open rebuke than a wedding.

Caleb had been a talented artist. In fact, he'd been accepted to one of the most prestigious art colleges in the nation. He showed us his drawings, and they were graphic, darkly disturbing, filled with many nude and violent images, but extremely talented nonetheless. So, we praised him for his talent. After all, he wasn't a disciple yet, and therefore not subject to the mandates of the anointing. Also, we all could legitimately appreciate his potential. He was also very openly sexual, based on his conversations with me. This was something I'd never been, and it kind of made me respect him. I'd always attempted to suppress my sexuality, which only worked for a time. This is not healthy. In fact, even the community teaches that you should be open about your thoughts, even sexual thoughts, as long as your openness is with the right person. So, for example, if I'd told Soreph Gamaliel when he sat down and talked to me about the race of my future wife, that I'd been entertaining lustful fantasies, it would have been completely appropriate. If, however, I would have told his wife or daughter that I'd been having lustful fantasies, it would have been entirely inappropriate, and might even be enough to get me kicked out of the community. So, Caleb, being open with me about his sexuality was something that the community would have seen as a good thing, and it is the same, in the community's belief, as being open with Yahshua.

Caleb's parents did get baptized in Hiddenite, and I would later hear of Caleb's baptism, after I was sent back to California. Caleb, too, was sent to California, but he was to live in the Vista community, and I lived at the Morningstar Ranch. Caleb's artistic talents would indeed prove useful to the community, as he was responsible for much of the artwork in the deli in Vista. He painted a large mural on the wall in the deli's courtyard. My old friend Elkanah, who'd lived with me in Missouri and in Vista, was also a talented artist and contributed to the Yellow Deli's artwork.

5

A FARMER'S DESTINY

My time in Hiddenite had been brief, only lasting for one growing season, but I got to do what I was passionate about, and I was free to unleash my creativity into my work. This was something rare for my experiences in the community. My garden had been successful too, and it felt good to have fed so many people. This was really the most powerful motivating factor for me, unlike other farmers I would encounter.

One evening, the leaders from the community in Hillsboro, Virginia came to Hiddenite and gave a presentation about their farm. Their presentation was a proud, and in my opinion at the time, arrogant display of agri-business, which had nothing to do with the anointing on farming. They were bragging about the acres of tomatoes they were growing and packaging for Whole Foods, and the hundreds of turkeys they slaughtered and sold on a daily basis. Meanwhile, the other communities in the tribe of Benjamin were buying food from Whole Foods. So, what profit had been made? The Hillsboro farm worked hard to produce food that got sold, and of course Whole Foods paid as little as they could get away with (because that's the nature of business), and meanwhile, the other communities worked hard in other ways to make money, and they bought produce from Whole Foods, and of course, Whole Foods charged as much as they could get away with. (This was before Amazon bought Whole Foods.) So, viewing all of the communities as one body, as we were taught to do, this was a wasteful practice. In fact, there were teachings about tribal trading, which was the practice of each community sharing its abundance with other communities and in that way, every community would have plenty of everything instead of an abundance of only a few things and a shortage of other things—kind of like the story of Stone Soup, but on a much larger scale.

This whole display had gotten me so worked up that I sat down that night and wrote a paper, which I called, "The Three Lifetime Destinies of Farmers." It was a categorization of farmers, much like the categorizations in The Three Eternal Destinies teachings. In my paper, there were the holy, the righteous, and the filthy-and-unjust farmers. The community believed in growing food organically, so naturally, the righteous and holy farmers both grew their crops organically, whereas the conventional farmers were in the filthy-and-unjust category. The difference between the righteous and the holy was that the righteous would certify their crops as organic and sell them at an organic premium, thus profiting from their crops. For farmers who were alone, or trying to run a business, this would be a perfectly reasonable thing to do. However, the holy should have no reason to certify their crops as organic, because they were growing food for the purpose of feeding their brothers and sisters. They still grew their food organically, it just wouldn't have been necessary for them to go through the certification process. Also, after feeding the community, they would bring their excess to farmer's markets and it would be both an opportunity to fund their farming operations and an opportunity to meet people in the hopes of converting new disciples. All of this, except for the bit about certification, had also been in-line with the anointing on farming, which layed-out the pattern for farms in the community. The fact that there would be no need for certification was a conclusion I'd come to, based on those teachings.

The pattern was simple: A cluster of communities would be established, with some communities operating farms, some cafés, and some working on various jobs and cottage industries to earn money. The farms were responsible for feeding their local cluster of communities, and if there was an abundance of something, whether it was something that was produced by the farm or by the cottage industry, they'd share that abundance with other clusters and those clusters in turn would share their abundance. The teachings also spoke of farmer's markets being a good way to evangelize and earn a little bit of cash for the farm. Agri-business was not part of this, and in fact, the teachings specifically mentioned agri-business as being a distraction from this pattern, and that making money should not be a primary focus of the community's farms. The farms were to be funded by those communities that were given the responsibility of making money, such as the communities that worked on various jobs or operated cottage industries. So, the natural conclusion was that certification would not be necessary if the communities were following this established pattern, as described in the anointing.

The next morning, I had given my paper to Soreph Gamaliel. He typed it up and distributed it to a few of the farmers who'd come to Hiddenite. One of these farmers, named Shoer, was very offended by the paper and wasted no time in letting me know how he felt. Zerubbabel had also read it, and he and Soreph had both liked it, but when I asked about how Yonéq had felt about it, I was told that Yonéq was not the king and that ultimately, it was up to all the farmers to decide.

I moved back to California along with Soreph Gamaliel and his family. Three days later, it was announced that Hadassah would also be moving back to California and she'd be living in the same community as me. This time, I'd felt that something was definitely going on. This couldn't be just a coincidence that she was moving all the way across the country right after I did, and then back again, right after I'd come back. I'd asked Mevaser about it and he told me, "I thought

I'd made it clear that the waiting period was over." Okay, so it was clear: It was over. I didn't like it, but at that point I just dealt with it and I stopped thinking about her and the possibility of her being my wife.

My time at the Morningstar Ranch can be summed up in two words: "Pain" and "Sacrifice." I was once again a training teacher, but I also worked in the garden, picked avocadoes on the avocado mountain the community owned, picked grapefruits and persimmons, milked cows and goats, and submitted to people who were clearly less experienced than I was. There was this grumpy old man from Boston, given the Hebrew name, "Reyah," who was heading-up the garden. I'd offered him a few suggestions as to how the garden could be a little bit more efficient, and he didn't seem to appreciate what I had to say. He got offended and went to some of the other brothers. They rebuked me and told me I was being strong and opinionated. Like always, I humbled myself and repented to him. I gave up my opinions, kept on working, and kept my mouth shut. My suggestions were right though. One of the things I'd said was that the overhead sprinklers were wasting water, which was not a good idea in California's desert climate. I suggested switching over to drip irrigation instead.

Not long after this, a man named Yathed, along with his family, was sent to the ranch from the community in Germany. Yathed was considered "the apostle of farming" by the leaders of the community.

Yathed had a lot of input for every aspect of the farm. The first thing he'd said about the garden was that we should switch to drip irrigation. Reyah, of course, acted like he'd never heard of this thing "drip irrigation" before. After a while of being treated like this, I decided that I was cut-off, not in fellowship with the community. When I was finally ready to humble myself and repent, I was told by Mevaser that there was one more thing I needed to repent for before I could be washed: He'd said that Shoer, from the tribe of Benjamin had talked to him about me, and that I was strongly opinionated about organic certification and that I should repent for trying to teach the community against certification. I repented and was washed. Not long after this, Shoer left the community and the entire farm in Hillsboro had been rebuked for their farming practices that went against the anointing. They didn't agree with my conclusion about certification being unnecessary, but that wasn't the main point I was hoping to make. The main point was that our purpose for farming should have been feeding people, not agri-business, and that was the point on which I was ultimately vindicated.

As it turned out, Yathed and I got along great. He and his family had been a breath of fresh air for me. I often worked with his younger son, Darush, who was this stereotypically chubby, clumsy, blonde, German boy who drooled a lot, and spit when he talked. He taught me how to say, "Ap-fel-Stru-dell", and I told him to remind me to bring an umbrella if I ever go to Germany (for the spittle). We each thought the other one was hilarious. Yathed had a lot of great ideas for the garden and had taught me quite a bit. Reyah had been a tennis pro from Boston who'd known nothing about gardening and who'd come into the community after me, but Yathed had been a farmer in the community for decades, so he was easy to listen to.

The hardest part for me at the Morningstar Ranch, other than the constant health issues I experienced (and the old men farting and snoring in the yurts, who'd get up at night and pee in jars right next to my head, even though there were plenty of trees outside to pee on), had been that at the end of a long day of work, I was often asked to watch multiple children. There was this tradition in the community called "family night." I'd always thought it was ironically named, because it was a night for married couples to push their children onto someone else and spend alone time together. They were served a separate meal, away from the rest of the community, which included desert, and then they spent the whole night together, without their children. So, it was basically just a date night. I was always so tired, but I did my best to care for all the children on the farm and people recognized that about me, so I was always the only single brother, out of the twenty-or-so on the farm, to be consistently asked to watch children. I once complained to the sister who was organizing these family nights. I was feeling dead-tired and she came to me and asked if I could watch the children, and when I'd asked her why none of the other twenty single brothers could do it, her response was, "Nobody else can read these children a story and tuck them into bed at night. Look at them!" Pointing to the yurts the brothers stayed in, she added, "Who would you want tucking in your children? Reyah?" I'd thought about it for a quick second and realized, not only was Reyah a complete dumbass, he was also a creepy old man, as were most of the other single brothers there. It was at that point I realized what was going on: These people weren't intentionally torturing me. They *needed* me.

I'd thought about my dad a lot, growing up without him. He'd been with lots of different women and had lots of children whom he didn't help raise. Here I was, single, a virgin, and caring for all these children that weren't mine. I was doing a damn good job at it too! I would often have several children working alongside me in the garden and then I'd go to the schoolhouse (the Morningstar Ranch had an actual schoolhouse on it) to teach classes. Then I'd go right back to work in the garden, the orchards, or the avocado mountain—wherever I was sent. I used to tell the children stories at night and I always made it entertaining. I would tell the stories with passion, and some humor. I had become a lot like Paul, my role model. He lived in the same community at the time, but interestingly, the longer I lived with him and the more I became like him, the smaller his stature became in my mind. He'd been a giant to me before, but now, here I was, looking after the children—even his children, in the same way he would have. Except that I wasn't married like he was, and none of these children were mine, so arguably, I should have had less motivation than him. I didn't have less motivation though. I did it for love, and it was true love, because I didn't expect anything for it.

During this time, Hadassah, who'd become an afterthought for me, had grown very cold towards me, to the point of becoming mean. She'd been given the position of kitchen covering, so she was in charge of all the community's food. There was a serious lack of protein on the ranch, because most of the animals we raised were not raised for their meat, and there just wasn't enough to go around. There were times we had avocados, but even those were being sold-off to the point of creating scarcity within the community. Sickle cell, being an anemia, requires a good, steady diet of protein and nutrient-rich foods. Especially given all the energy I was expelling with my daily activities—I had a great need. One morning, I'd asked Hadassah for a second helping of porridge for breakfast. It was a real-life Oliver Twist scene. She had half a pot left, but she wouldn't give me any more. I was lagging while working in the garden and one of the shepherds asked me what was wrong, so I told him. He marched right back up to the kitchen, which was a good hike away from the garden, and he rebuked Hadassah for not giving me enough food. He brought me some more food and it never happened again after that.

Since the Morningstar Ranch was on the side of an avocado mountain, with all the buildings being at the base, it was easy to get exhausted walking up and down a hill every day. I'd wake up at five in the morning and walk downhill from the yurts to the barn to milk the animals, then walk back uphill and get ready for the gathering. Then I'd walk down to the gathering which was sometimes inside the schoolhouse and sometimes just outside, then walk back up to the main house to eat breakfast, then walk down to the garden, then back up to the schoolhouse, up to lunch at the main house, down to the garden, up the avocado mountain, down to the barn for evening milking, back up to the yurts, down to the gathering, up to the house, and by the time I would get to bed after tucking the children in, it'd be about ten, and the next morning I'd have to do it all over again—six days per week. Being on my feet for sixteen to seventeen hours and constantly hiking like that was my daily routine.

The fences at the ranch were also a big issue. I had to repair a lot of temporary fences and couldn't figure out why they couldn't just spring for the one-time expense of a more permanent solution. The bull would often get out and they'd come to me to get him back in. He was a big, rowdy, Jersey bull. I'd grab a bucket of grain and start shaking it at him and then he'd run straight for me, so I'd run too— right into his pen. He'd chase me in there and I'd whip around and run right back out the gate, shutting it behind me. One time, I didn't run fast enough and he penned me against the metal wire fence. I grabbed his horns and he jerked his neck real hard and slammed me into the fence, leaving a big dent. I got loose though, and got him to chase me back in his pen. One Friday, which was the day the community fasted until late in the afternoon, I'd been given the job of setting up an electric fence. These were the fences I really hated, because they always seemed to require so much maintenance. It was me and a boy, about the age of twelve, and we had to dig a bunch of fence post holes first, then put in some eight-foot cedar posts. We installed all the insulators and ran all the wires. It surrounded about an acre of pasture. It was almost the Sabbath (Sabbath starts at sunset, Friday night), but we had to finish up so we could let the animals out of the barn and into the pasture. We finished right in time to get ready quickly for the gathering. I'd tested the fence and it shocked me, so I knew it was working, but then the stubborn donkey (the only donkey we had on the farm) got its ankle tangled in the wire and started kicking. It yanked a long strand of wire loose, breaking the circuit. All of the animals escaped, so this boy and I had to spend all of preparation hour fixing the wire and rounding-up the animals. The real kicker was, I'd gotten called-out for it at the gathering that night, for dishonoring the Sabbath by showing up late. It still sucked to have to go through all that stress to help the entire community only to be shamed for it at the evening gathering. I wasn't seeking praise, but I certainly didn't deserve to be publicly humiliated for my efforts.

That stubborn donkey—we got rid of it, but there was a time when I was in charge of it. I couldn't ride it downhill, I'd found out. Once, I tried riding it down to the garden and it started galloping and then kicked its back legs up, flipping me forward. As I was falling, I thought, "It's going to trample me, for sure." But it had come to an abrupt stop, so I said, "Thank you Abba," as I slammed to the ground, flat on my back. Even so, for a time, it had been useful to me. I could ride it up the avocado mountain. Every other man on the farm would have two bags slung across each opposing shoulder, so the straps would make an x-shape on their front and back (I'd done this for a time too). They'd fill the bags up, then walk back down the hill to a big, plastic crate that would get picked up by the tractor once it was full. But during the time I had the donkey, I typically had four bags, slung over the donkey's back. I'd fill up the bags, then walk the donkey down the hill to those plastic crates and empty my bags. We had to get rid of the donkey though, because I got sick too often and nobody else wanted to take care of it.

There was a man named Nathan who had come into the community during my time at the ranch. He was tall and strong. He was a big, ugly brute of a guy and he liked to talk a lot in the gatherings, even before he was baptized. He had a way of moving his arms up and down rapidly as he spoke, and much of what he said sounded like he was trying to teach everybody. To the community, it was kind of off-putting when someone new tried to teach. I remember the night of his baptism painfully well. It was a typically hot Southern California day, so I was wearing a short-sleeved shirt. The sun hadn't yet set when we gathered, but this man, Nathan, started speaking and it was pitch black out before he was done. We were gathered outside, but there was a circle of lights strung-up for such occasions. Being a desert climate, the temperature dropped rapidly when the sun went down, but this man was about to be baptized, so I couldn't be disrespectful and leave to put on a long-sleeved shirt or a jacket.

That night, I'd had severe sickle cell pain in my arms. I laid in my bunk all night in agony and by the next morning I was shaking profusely and vomiting. I asked to go to the hospital that day. I was hospitalized for more than a week. By the time I recovered, Nathan had become a crew head. He was Shem after all (a white man), and he was a natural-born leader. Nathan pushed me hard, whether it was hiking the mountain to pick avocados, or digging ditches, picking grapefruits, he was zealous about all the work that needed to get done and he knew how to push people. I think that's why the leaders liked him so much—he made things happen and they didn't seem to care how. He was not a friendly leader. One rainy night, Nathan came into the yurt and demanded that all the brothers come outside and help him dig ditches. I refused. I explained to him that I have sickle cell and cannot work outside in the cold and wet—that it would cause another crisis. He yelled at me for a good while and I just kept saying, "no." Finally, Nathan went and got one of the older leaders. When the two men came back in to talk to me about it, I explained the situation to them logically. "How will you explain my death to the world (outsiders)?" That had been the end of the conversation and I slept well that night.

Nathan and Hadassah went on a waiting period not long after he joined the community and they were eventually married. They were perfect for each other.

I had three separate sickle cell crises requiring hospitalization while living at the Morningstar Ranch. One of those times had clearly been my fault, but the consequences of my actions had been severe. I'd given into peer pressure and jumped into one of the ponds that the community used for swimming. It had been a warm day and everyone kept saying, "C'mon you can't even take a dip? It's so warm out." I felt fine at first, and I even told one of the girls who knew about my condition that I had gone swimming. She looked concerned, but I said I felt fine. Then a wave of pain hit me as I walked away.

By the time I changed out of my wet clothes, I was writhing in agony. I believe it was the first time I'd thought about the lake of fire while I was having a crisis. I was sure that this must be what the lake of fire feels like.

I made my way down the driveway towards one of the houses, but I collapsed and fell into a lavender bush. I laid there struggling, trying to gain control of my breathing, while the smell of lavender overwhelmed my sinuses. This had been the worst pain I'd ever experienced. Once, not that long ago, I'd sat down on the Sabbath outside the yurt and cut-off the top half of my big toenail because it had become ingrown. I'd cut the nail with a razor blade then yanked it off my toe. I found out that day that there are a lot of nerves underneath toenails, but the pain had been a one on a scale of one to ten. This pain I was experiencing now, my head in a lavender bush, imagining the lake of fire, was a ten. One of the women saw me and ran to get a couple brothers to help me. They made a bed for me inside Darush and his brother's room, which was warm, because it was inside the house where the married couples and their children lived. Mevaser came and prayed for me. I felt cold and numb. I knew for certain that God was taking me away. It's odd though, the thought I had on my death bed wasn't about Heaven. I just regretted not having done more in my life. I thought about all the times I'd gotten self-conscious and how silly that seemed now. How insignificant my ego was in the sight of death! I'd held back for no reason, held back from passionately sharing my heart in the gathering, held back from singing with all my heart, held back from saying whatever I felt like saying. Why? Why had I held back so much when life is so short? I wondered what my mark on the world would be.

I spent another eight days or so in the hospital and I did get better. Many people resented the fact that I was going to the hospital so often. "Are you trying to bankrupt the Twelve Tribes?" one brother had asked. I convinced the leaders that perhaps the best thing for my

130

health would be to send me back to Missouri. So, in the summer of 2010, I ended up right back where I started five years earlier—at the Stepping Stone Farm, in Weaubleau, Missouri.

It was a hot night in June when I got back to the farm in Weaubleau. The humidity was comforting for me, after experiencing those nightly drops in temperature at the Morningstar Ranch. Daveed had picked me up from the airport in Kansas City. There were a lot more people living on the farm than when I'd first lived there. It wasn't just that there were more people, but there were also a lot more families on the farm than when I'd lived there before, so that meant a lot more children to care for.

Though there were plenty of people on the farm now, Daveed and his family were the only people I knew, so it had a completely different feel. Yahalom had left the community, as had my shepherd, Ben Shimon. I had been devastated, hearing about their departures. They had broken their covenant. Others had merely been sent to different communities. Reshef and Amanah's family, as well as Naboth and Eshet, had moved to the Warsaw community. As odd as it was to be in this familiar place with so many unfamiliar faces, I felt comfortable enough with the new folks on the farm. They were, after all, disciples of Yahshua, so it wasn't hard to get to know them.

There was a man living on the farm named Yohanan. We called him Yohanan Patman, because there were a lot of other Yohanans in the Twelve Tribes and his last name happened to be Patman. Yohanan Patman looked and sounded like if Ned Flanders from The Simpson's had been a real person, but with a beard and pony tail. It was easy to get along with him. He'd been the rabbi at that community, and he was also attempting to grow the garden that year with just the help of the children, so he was relieved when I showed up to help. I put my knowledge to good use. All the things Yathed had taught me came in handy and we ended up with such a productive garden that it fed our community, the Warsaw community, and we even had enough produce left over for Yohanan and me to go to the Bolivar farmer's markets once a week.

The only other single brother there at that time was Zachai. He was also easy to get along with. It was a lot easier to share a room with just one other guy than with twenty. Zachai was a tough guy that had been in prison before joining the community. He was muscular and had a bunch of tattoos, but now he was a sensitive, gentle giant of a man. He wasn't that tall, only average height, but giant in the sense that he was solidly-built. He and I would often be sent evangelizing, and that was always a good experience. We'd go up to Kansas City or St. Louis and hand out freepapers together. It felt good to spend time with someone I got along with and tell other people about the community, but I also liked it because it was the one time when I could get some coffee. The community didn't allow daily coffee drinking, but they said that if you were on a road trip, you could stop for coffee to stay awake so you could be safe.

That fall, Yohanan Patman announced in a gathering that he'd been speaking with a man named Edward, from Oklahoma, who was interested in joining the community. Yohanan said he'd be picking him up from the bus station. Edward, from Oklahoma? It sounded oddly familiar to me. Sure enough, Yohanan had come back with my old friend, Joshua Charles Edward North III. He'd said he didn't want to be called Charles, because that was his father's name and his father had been drunk and abusive, so he asked to be called Edward instead, and the community obliged.

This time around, Edward and I really didn't get along at all. He was no less religious (in the mystical and hypocritical sense of the word), than he'd been before, and he hadn't given up his intense envy towards me. He seemed focused on me, watching my every move and waiting for me to mess up. He'd often try to rebuke me for stuff I'd say that he thought was wrong, based on his religion, and I wasn't having it. We ended up in a few meetings and they always ended with Edward getting corrected by the leaders, because the things I'd said were perfectly in-line with the anointing. He'd have to repent to me, and I could tell he really hated it. Edward lasted about six months. The last straw, for us, not for him, had been an incident that had occurred one cold day, in the early spring, when all the brothers had been called upon to help at a construction site.

Shomer, who was one of Naboth and Eshet's older sons, was a general contractor. Although Naboth and Eshet were living in the Warsaw community at the time, Shomer was living on the farm and leading construction jobs. Zachai would often help him, along with another man named Boaz. This time, though, they needed all the men to help. They'd been doing some framing for a large garage or warehouse-type building. They built the walls on the ground and they needed all of us to help raise them. When we were raising one of the walls, it started falling back on us. Someone said, "We are so stupid!" as it started falling on us. Then someone else shouted, "Abba help us!" We pushed with all our might and got that wall up. That night at the gathering, everyone was giving thanks to our Father for protection and then Edward decided to speak up. He said that he could just feel our Father lifting the wall up for us. Then he said, "At one point I just let go—just a little bit…" He was smiling as he said this, looking upwards toward his god in heaven, and putting his hands flat together as Christians often do when they pray. "I prayed to God and He lifted up that wall for us!" he said.

The community believed that this type of behavior (putting your brothers' lives at risk by letting go of a wall, even if just a little bit) was from an evil spirit. More specifically, it is the same evil spirit they recognize in religion, which causes people to not consider their own deeds, because they are more concerned about their faith and about being saved. Indeed, it is one of the things I most dislike about religion. It seems to be filled with hypocrisy, when it should be filled with people who are constantly looking out for other people's needs.

The community did not consider themselves to be part of Christianity in any way. They made several distinctions between themselves and mainstream Christianity. Not the least of which is the distinction between Christianity's insistence on salvation being based only on faith, not by deeds. The community of course, believes that deeds are far more important, because it is through your deeds that you prove your faith and by your deeds that you will be judged. So crucial are these distinctions, that the community came to the conclusion that Christianity is Babylon, and the harlot, from Revelation 17 and 18:

The woman was clothed in purple and scarlet, and adorned with gold and precious stones and pearls,

having in her hand a gold cup full of abominations and of the unclean things of her immorality,

and on her forehead a name was written, a mystery, "BABYLON THE GREAT, THE MOTHER OF HARLOTS AND OF THE ABOMINATIONS OF THE EARTH."

Fallen, fallen is Babylon the great! She has become a dwelling place of demons and a prison of every unclean spirit, and a prison of every unclean and hateful bird.

For all the nations have drunk of the wine of the passion of her immorality, and the kings of the earth have committed acts of immorality with her,

and the merchants of the earth have become rich by the wealth of her sensuality.

Come out of her, my people, so that you will not participate in her sins and receive of her plagues;

for her sins have piled up as high as heaven, and God has remembered her iniquities.

Pay her back even as she has paid, and give back to her double according to her deeds; in the cup which she has mixed, mix twice as much for her.

To the degree that she glorified herself and lived sensuously, to the same degree give her torment and mourning; for she says in her heart,

'I sit as a queen and I am not a widow, and will never see mourning.'

For this reason in one day her plagues will come, pestilence and mourning and famine, and she will be burned up with fire; for the Lord God who judges her is strong.

The reasoning behind this assertion was that "the first church" fell away from the true faith and the Holy Spirit was not on the earth for 1900 years, until Yonéq came along and he and his wife established the Twelve Tribes Communities. The community used this term "first church" to refer to the community churches described in the book of Acts, while mainstream Christians tend to refer to it as "the early church," because this falling away from faith is not a commonly accepted doctrine in mainstream Christianity. However, there are a few verses in the Bible which seem to support this doctrine:

> But I have this against you, that you have left your first love.
>
> Therefore remember from where you have fallen, and repent and do the deeds you did at first;
>
> or else I am coming to you and will remove your lampstand out of its place—unless you repent. (Rev. 2:4-5)
>
> What use is it, my brethren, if someone says he has faith but he has no works? Can that faith save him?
>
> If a brother or sister is without clothing and in need of daily food, and one of you says to them, "Go in peace, be warmed and be filled," and yet you do not give them what is necessary for their body, what use is that?
>
> Even so faith, if it has no works, is dead, being by itself.
>
> But someone may well say, "You have faith and I have works; show me your faith without the works, and I will show you my

faith by my works."

You believe that God is one. You do well; the demons also believe, and shudder.

But are you willing to recognize, you foolish fellow, that faith without works is useless?

Was not Abraham our father justified by works when he offered up Isaac his son on the altar? You see that faith was working with his works, and as a result of the works, faith was perfected;

and the Scripture was fulfilled which says, "And Abraham believed God, and it was reckoned to him as righteousness," and he was called the friend of God.

You see that a man is justified by works and not by faith alone. In the same way, was not Rahab the harlot also justified by works when she received the messengers and sent them out by another way?

For just as the body without the spirit is dead, so also faith without works is dead. (James 2:14-16)

The community taught that the lampstand of Revelation 2:5 was taken away, not to be restored again until the Twelve Tribes Communities were established. At one point, the churches did live communally, just as the modern-day Twelve Tribes do, but they left their first love and they stopped caring for the needy. For this reason, the community believes that the sins of Christianity have been piling-up for about 1,900 years and that they will be judged harshly for this at the end of the age. This judgement is for the institution of Christianity, but individuals will be judged based on their works. There was even a teaching in which Yonéq said, "Just because you are a Christian doesn't necessarily mean that you are going to the lake of fire." He went on to explain that it is by their deeds that the people of the nations will be judged, not by their religion. "The nations" was another expression that the community used to refer to those who were not part of the community.

It was clear to everyone in the community at the time, that Edward was under the influence of these Christian spirits, which caused him to have a mystical perspective on life, ignoring reality to the point of putting others in danger. He left shortly after that incident. I'm not sure if he'd been asked to leave, if he wanted to leave, or both. Probably both. Either way, he learned that if he wanted to be in the community he had to give up Christianity. It was made very clear to him, and he ultimately chose Christianity.

Zachai was sent to California, to the Morningstar Ranch, so with he and Edward gone, I was the only single brother left on the farm. With the spring planting season approaching, I once again turned my attention towards the garden. Yohanan had made a wise investment, purchasing an old Ford 8N tractor for just $1,200. It worked like a champ and I drove that thing all over the farm, hauling stuff on the hay wagons, cultivating the garden, and raking hay. I even drove it down to our farm stand with a wagon full of straw bales and produce. I was very productive during that time, and it gave me something to focus on to take my mind off of girls.

Later that spring, a girl showed up. Her name was Caitlin, and she'd been a WOOFer too, travelling to various organic farms, working in exchange for room-and-board. She looked like she was maybe in her mid-forties the day she arrived. Travelling had been hard on her. Her sandy-blonde hair was dirty and natty looking, and her face looked old, worn and wrinkly. Her eyes were droopy and sad, but she was smiling nonetheless, happy to have arrived at yet another destination of many. It was almost as if The Stepping Stone Farm was just a stepping stone for her, rather than a home. There was nothing binding her there and she could have left at any time without anyone trying too hard to convince her otherwise. There would be no hurt feelings or crying, no accusations that she was breaking her covenant, or threats of death, or an eternity in the lake of fire. The community could just say their goodbyes as she left, if that's what she chose to do. She was completely free, and in that I envied her.

Not long before I'd left the Morningstar Ranch, I'd thought a lot about leaving the community, but didn't quite know how I'd go about accomplishing such a feat. Then something happened that had both saddened and terrified all of us. A man by the name of Ryan, who'd partially grown up in the community at the Basin Farm, but had left, decided to come back. He was baptized and lived with us at the Ranch, and then at the Vista community. While he was there, an old friend decided to visit him. Apparently, they'd known each other since childhood and she had left the community too. She was married now, but she still wanted to see Ryan. He'd been working late at the deli in Vista and the brothers told us he was probably tired and vulnerable. For whatever reason, they'd left together. She was driving, and while travelling north on I-5, she must have dozed-off. She crossed the median and hit head-on with an oncoming semi-truck. They were both killed instantly. The brothers determined that it was our Father's judgment, and that it was a lesson to all of us: If you leave the place of our father's protection, there is no guarantee that you will be protected.

I had been terrified, but guests like Caitlin had no such fears, and indeed she was a free-spirited individual. For whatever reason, the community decided it would be a good idea if she worked with me in the garden, instead of with the women in the house. I was not happy with the arrangement at first and I voiced my frustration to Yohanan, telling him how awkward it felt. He reminded me that it wasn't about me. She was a WOOFer, a willing worker on an organic farm. She wasn't here to cook and clean. She wanted to learn about farming, and I'd been taught by the best. So, Caitlin worked along-side of me and I taught her some of what I knew.

After a day or two, she'd been given an opportunity to get plenty of rest and looked ten years younger, but she was still dirty all the time, which was fitting for the job. After the first week, Caitlin showed up at the Friday night celebration and she was glowing. Someone must have told her how special that night was to us, because she really cleaned up. She was wearing a new dress that one of the women must have given her. It was a very contrasting look for her, compared to the dirty jeans I'd seen her in the rest of the week. Her hair was all done-up too and it looked a lot lighter, probably because she'd washed all the dirt out. I was sitting across the circle from her and she kept smiling at me.

The next week, as we worked together in the garden, Caitlin started talking about wanting to go out into the wilderness, maybe in Utah. She thought Utah seemed like it would be a beautiful place. I hadn't told her anything about all the time I had spent fantasizing about living in the wilderness, completely free and independent, but here she was talking about it. I had always just accepted that I would never find a girl who would be willing to go out to the wilderness with me and live such an uncomfortable life, but here was this young, twenty-something woman (she actually looked her age now after re-covering from the wearies of travelling), across the garden bed from me talking about going to the wilderness. She was squatting-down, wearing a loose t-shirt and showing me her cleavage as she spoke. I told her I thought it was a bad idea, trying to live in the wilderness by herself. It was too dangerous. She needed someone with survival skills to come with her. "Would you like to go to the wilderness with me?" she asked, smiling up at me and kind of giggling a little.

I remember feeling that familiar, cruel pain I'd felt whenever Hadassah would smile at me. Beauty really was incredibly cruel. My first thought was, 'No! Of course not! I'm a disciple of Yahshua, and this would be such an incredibly selfish thing for a disciple of Yahshua to do,' but somehow what I said instead was a weak, "Yes."

I tried to pretend like nothing happened, like I hadn't majorly fallen on my face when she asked me if I wanted to go to the wilderness with her. It was easy for her to move on, being the free spirit she was, but I was a disciple and I knew this had been a huge slip-up. I was a complete hypocrite in my own eyes, but I could tell she didn't see me as such. She saw me as just a normal young man with normal desires. Over the next week or so, Caitlin began asking a series of questions pertaining to relationships between men and women in the community. She asked, not just me, but others in the community as well. She told me she had asked one of the women if she was allowed to have a boyfriend in the community and they'd told her, "No." She asked me about it and I tried to explain the whole process, of waiting

143

periods, betrothals, and marriage. She said, "So, if I wanted to be with you, I'd have to get baptized first?" and I'd told her, "Yes."

The truth was, even if two people happen to like each other, even if they both want to be together, there's no guarantee that the community would put them together. The community would often separate people instead. It was all up to the married couples who participated in the social meetings to decide the fate of two young people who wanted to be together. After about three weeks of temptation and sexual frustration, Caitlin and I were planting in one of the back fields when we decided to take a walk together in the woods. We sat down, side-by-side on an old wooden platform someone had built for a tent. She asked me what I wanted to do and I knew she wasn't referring to just that moment. She was asking me to make a decision, to decide between her and the community. To me, at that time, it was as if I was being asked to choose between life and death, between God and the devil.

I remember looking up at the trees and sensing angels looking back down at me, through the walls of another dimension, waiting for me to decide. I felt like it was one more great temptation for me to overcome. At the same time, I really didn't know what to believe anymore. Nothing seemed real to me anymore except for this living, breathing woman who was sitting right next to me. I could feel her warmth. Our hips were touching. And the angels in the other dimension, whom I couldn't even see or touch, weren't so real to me. So, I put my hand on Caitlin's back, and I said, "I've made my decision." We talked a little bit about what we would do, and I said I'd get a job. She told me not to get a job, that she would take care of me, though I wasn't sure how and I was even less sure about how we'd go about actually leaving the community. I was also worried about hurting so many people who had come to rely on me. It was at that time I remembered Ryan, and how he died.

I walked back towards the houses and I saw Daveed, who was just finishing with the milking chores. I confessed to him what had happened, about talking to Caitlin in the woods and putting my hand on her back. I'd never seen him so angry before. He threw the milk bucket down and walked off, towards the dirt road. I didn't really know what to do at that point. I started to follow him, but it seemed he needed some time alone. I watched him walk down the road, beyond the edge of our property. He was looking upwards and saying something, so I could tell he was probably praying. He'd later told me he wasn't angry at me, but he was angry at himself and at the other shepherds for letting me down by not paying close enough attention to what was going on, and for not listening to me when I'd told them I was uncomfortable working with Caitlin. In all honesty, it had been a while since I'd complained about working with her, because I'd grown to love it.

I knew I was cut off at that time, so I showed up to the gathering without my diadem on, which was how the community knew whether you were connected or cut off. A diadem is a headband that was worn by royalty so that their heads wouldn't get cut by their crown. The community members wore linen diadems to the gatherings as a symbol of their expected future coronation by the Messiah when He returned. Women wore their diadems over their head coverings, but men just wore them as head bands. So, those who were cut off were not allowed to wear their diadems or head coverings, and they were not allowed to lift their hands with everyone else during the prayer at the end of the gathering. In practical terms, this served as a way to publicly shame and disgrace those who were not in unity with the rest of the community.

After the gathering, there was a long judgment meeting, in which all the brothers attempted to judge me spiritually, and to give me advice. Of course, Caitlin, being a guest, was not subject to such judgments, so she was not present at this meeting. I'd been brutally honest with them about everything that was going on with me. I confessed everything and left nothing hidden. I was re-connected after the meeting. Caitlin and I continued to live in the same community for the next few weeks, but she worked alongside the other women during that time. She'd told them that she wanted to be baptized and eventually she convinced the whole community that her desire to be a disciple was sincere, and she was baptized in the waters of Pomme de Terre Lake.

Not long after Caitlin's baptism, it was decided that I would be sent to live in the community in Warsaw. I'd asked Yohanan Patman how long I'd have to stay in Warsaw and he'd told me, "Until the leaves change color." It was early summer at the time, so I'd assumed that meant I'd only have to be separated from Caitlin for a few months and then we could go on a waiting period.

6

A YOUNG SPROUT IN A ROCKY PLACE

Moving to Warsaw was devastating for me. Not only was it difficult being separated from this beautiful young woman who actually liked me, but now I had nothing to distract me from the pain. Farming had become my life, and now here I was, in a "city" community. My fate was to become a training teacher once again, and also to work in the café. My daily routine, after the morning gathering, was to teach training until around 2pm and then walk down to the café and work late into the night. Unlike farming, these were duties that required me to maintain my spiritual connection at all times, because whatever spirit I was in communion with would be passed on to the children, and of course, I'd only want to teach them according to the Holy Spirit. It was important to maintain this spiritual connection at the café, because there I was representing our life to the nations. Maintaining such a connection to the community was not as easy as it may sound, because unlike other religions, it was not simply a personal connection. It wasn't as simple as praying to Jesus and being forgiven.

In the community, you were expected to exercise self-control in all aspects of your life—your thoughts, words, actions, and even your social interactions with others. You were expected to maintain unity with every other disciple at all times if you were to maintain communion with the Holy Spirit. From this, there were no distractions. There was no easy way out once you were placed in such a position. Not if you cared about the people you affected.

There was another Yohanan in the Warsaw community. He was about sixteen-years-old. His name was Ian, the son of Mark and Jennifer, but now he was Yohanan, the son of Reshef and Amanah. The once dweeby little boy who wanted to be an archeologist was now a loyal disciple of Yahshua and a talented guitar player. He and another boy about the same age looked a lot like younger versions of John Lennon and Paul McCartney as they played music in the gathering. They wore their guitars low on their waists, swaying and grooving with careless ease as they played. I liked their laid-back style and how they seemed to not possess an ounce of self-consciousness. Yohanan had come a long way, and as it turned out, we got along well and spent quite a bit of time together. We even wrote a play together once, which we performed at a Bar Mitzvah, with help from other members of the community.

The person I'd spent the most time with was a man named Tamiym. He was about the same age as me, though much taller, and the fact that he had a beard and I could not grow one made him look older. He was a blonde man from Minnesota and I suspect he was of Viking heritage. I'm not sure if I would have made it through my time in Warsaw had it not been for Tamiym. I probably would have given up and just walked off, with nothing to my name and nowhere to go. I would have wandered off into the woods somewhere without the will to live, and I'm not sure where I'd be now if that had happened, or even if I'd still be alive. What I liked most about Tamiym was that he was always so real about everything. If he was having a hard time, he wasn't afraid to show it. He struggled a lot, but you could tell he wanted to be faithful. He was his own worst critic, but he was always forgiving of others when their faults were clearly far worse than his. People like that are the opposite of religious hypocrites, even when they see themselves as such. It was easy for me to open up to Tamiym about my own struggles when he was always so open to me.

Tamiym had a wife named Elah, and he and his wife, along with Yohanan and I, had been sent to a music festival once. It was called Wakarusa. We'd driven down to Arkansas and camped by a River. Tamiym was making us laugh the whole time with his goofy sense of humor.

We drove through the town of Huntsville, with its bland, brick buildings, and typical, bleak, small town America feel. We probably wouldn't have remembered the town at all, had it not been for the fact that Tamiym blurted out, "Well this is an awkward town!" as we passed it. His comments somehow caught us off guard every time.

When we got to the music festival, we all put on backpacks full of freepapers and somehow managed to just walk right through the gate without tickets. I'm pretty sure the tickets would have been more than we could have afforded, but we just walked right in instead. There were half-naked women everywhere and we had fun talking to them about the community. I felt perfectly comfortable with Tamiym and his wife and Yohanan. We were just a bunch of young people, having a good time and talking to folks.

One of my favorite memories from Warsaw was walking home from the café with Tamiym every work day. It was the best time to talk about stuff I wouldn't talk about with anyone else. It was never anything bad, just things I wouldn't want to say in front of the whole community. Living in a house full of people can feel emotionally claustrophobic at times, so it was nice to have someone to vent to. I'd vent to Tamiym and he'd vent to me; it was a symbiotic relationship.

Fall came and went with no word from the farm. There had been a few festivals and a Bar Mitzvah, which brought folks from the farm up to Warsaw. So I saw Caitlin, but I couldn't talk to her. I'd look over in her direction and she'd smile at me and then I'd have to look away. Then we'd have to go our separate ways. It hurt every time, but I did my best to focus on my spiritual life. I focused on the teachings and the word of God, and I tried my best to be faithful.

There was a series of teachings being taught to the whole Twelve Tribes during the time I was living in Warsaw. The teachings were based on a woman named Rakefet who'd lived in New England. She had lung cancer and it seemed she was dying. The doctors only gave her a few weeks to live, but she surpassed their expectations. Some of the members of the community who had medical experience were caring for her. The teachings went into detail about how grave her situation was. She had an open wound on her chest and they'd been using a salve made with black cohosh to treat it. They described how the once gaping wound was closing-up and where there was once rotten flesh, new life was growing. Supple, pink skin was filling the wound. Of course, all of this was used as an analogy for the community as a whole. A lot of people were struggling with their iniquities and a lot of people, even leaders, were leaving the community. Just as Rakefet was recovering, so too would the community, the body of the Messiah. We were instructed to pray for her continued recovery and for "the body" (the Twelve Tribes).

I watched a lot of sincere people pray for Rakefet, especially the other sisters. They'd pray, in tears, at the end of each gathering. A young man named Yachal, who lived in the Warsaw community, had gone out to New England and visited his mother, who had been one of the people caring for Rakefet. When he came back, he saw the people praying for her and afterwards he talked to some of the leaders. I happened to be sitting with them. Yachal asked the leaders if they knew Rakefet had died. They said they knew about it, but they were waiting to hear from Hiddenite as to how they should break the news to the community. They were unsure of the implications, given the teachings. Essentially, they did not want people to start questioning the legitimacy of the community based on the teachings about Rakefet. Since she'd been used as an analogy for the community, they did not want to tell people she was dead for fear they might think that the community was spiritually dead.

I was quiet over the next few weeks. We were expected to share what was on our hearts at the gatherings, but I didn't feel much like speaking. I watched helplessly as the women continued to pray for the recovery of their sister, oblivious to her passing. At times I wanted to shout, "This is bullshit!" I'd looked over at Yachal and he had the same expression. It wasn't long before he was gone. His father had already left the community, Yachal and his brothers followed, not far behind. I couldn't leave though. At least I didn't think I could. So, since I couldn't leave, I couldn't say anything. Criticizing the leaders was enough to get kicked out and I didn't think I had anywhere else to go. So, I just continued to watch helplessly for the next few weeks until the leaders finally decided to break the news.

I had a dream during that time. I was on the front porch of the house in Warsaw. It was a grand, southern-style porch, with tables for sitting and eating at in the summer. I was sitting at one of these tables across from an old lady. I'd told the woman that I wanted to marry her daughter. "You'd like to marry my daughter?" she'd asked. Then she motioned towards what appeared to be some sort of three-dimensional board game sitting on the table. The board was full of greenery, grass, flowers, and trees. There was a stone path, and on that path, were the names of each of the Twelve Tribes. The old lady handed me a stone, and she said, "If you would like to marry my daughter, then put this stone here." She pointed to the tribe of Yehudah. I put the stone in the place that had been designated for Yehudah, and Yehudah was gone. Dead. All the greenery around it had died too. She had me keep doing this, one stone at a time, and one tribe at a time, until I got to the tribe of Manasseh. That was my tribe, and I was weeping as I stuck the stone down over my tribe, killing it. But still, I kept going, until all the tribes had been killed, and the entire board had turned into a dry, cracked wasteland. There was nothing but dead, brown, thorny briars and dry, cracked earth. Black storm clouds gathered over the desert and lightning flashed violently and rapidly. The rain started pouring down and rivers started flowing. Then suddenly life burst forth onto the board and it was even more glorious than it had been before. The storm gave way to a rainbow. The thorns and briars disappeared and were replaced with green grass, shrubs, trees, and flowers everywhere. Flocks of birds flew out of the trees with such a loud noise that it woke me up. I woke up weeping, and I was sitting fully upright.

The rest of my time spent in the Warsaw community had been a desperate attempt to maintain my faith in God and my trust in the leaders, while trying not to think about Caitlin. She was sent to live in Colorado, but I was told that it was only temporary. When I asked the leaders about it, they told me she needed to be given a solid foundation. I had asked if that meant I'd be going back to the farm, seeing as the only reason I was sent to Warsaw in the first place was to be separated from her. They told me they'd talk about it.

I was sent back to the farm in March. Naboth and Eshet had also moved back to the farm. I was glad to be back, and I knew the last time I lived on the farm I had really messed up. I was thankful to be forgiven and ready to face the future, but that didn't last long.

Shortly after moving back to the farm, Yohanan from Warsaw showed up to a gathering one night, along with another young man. They said they were going to a Christian rock concert to evangelize. The brothers decided I should go with them, along with another man from the farm named Jehu, but we had to leave right away. It had been a warm day, so I was wearing a short-sleeved shirt, but it was also early spring, so the temperature dropped fast while we were out that night. I was sure that God had sent me, because after all, I was being obedient to my brothers and I had been sent to this event. It was our Father's will to evangelize. He wanted us to reach out to the Christians, because there were so many sincere people in that dead religion. They were deceived, and they needed to hear the true gospel. It was clear to me that this was God's will, and yet, the pain still came. I was still being punished, even though I was doing God's will. That night, during the ride home, the pain kept coming in waves, getting worse with each wave. I laid in bed all night, thinking about the lake of fire. I was sure that this must be what it would feel like. I couldn't imagine a worse pain. I'd asked God why I was being punished, but I didn't get an answer. There had never been an answer. All these circumstances had always been so random. It was at that time that I started to have legitimate doubts. It wasn't like before, where I'd simply struggle with my faith and then repent and move on. This time was much different. From that point on, I started to see everything differently.

Shortly after recovering from that episode, I was once again sent out to evangelize. This time it was to Kansas City, for the St. Patrick's Day celebrations. I went with Eved, the single brother I had spent the weekend with the first time I'd visited the Warsaw community. Only now he wasn't a single brother. He'd gotten married to a woman named Yasmine, who always seemed to be in a rotten mood. Her attitude was strikingly contrasting from what I was accustomed to encountering in the community, which was made especially odd by the fact that she'd grown up in the community, in the tribe of Yehudah.

She always seemed to have something to complain about, even though we were taught as disciples to never grumble or complain, but to always give thanks in all things. Eved, on the other hand, always seemed to be happy and thankful, but I don't think he even noticed his new wife's odd behavior. It was as if he was completely oblivious to it. So Eved and his wife had been sent, along with myself and a young woman named Molly, who was new to the community, to evangelize in Kansas City, on St. Patrick's Day.

The whole event had been a little odd. First, Eved decided to drive and his wife sat in the front passenger seat, leaving me and Molly, both of us single, to sit together in the back seat. Typically, the community went to great lengths to separate single brothers from single sisters, so that in itself was odd. But also, Molly was a new disciple, and yet here she was, being sent to a raucous, worldly celebration. Molly had been sent from the community in Colorado to live on the farm shortly before I moved back to the farm, and shortly after Caitlin had been sent to live in Colorado. So, I guess she was a trade-off for Caitlin. Molly was a bigger girl, thicker than the frail, occasionally even anorexic girls that I was used to encountering in the community. I think by comparison that made her seem even bigger than she actually was. The first thing I noticed about her, the first time I saw her, was how big her arms were. She could easily beat the crap out of me, if she really wanted to, and yet, she also seemed so vulnerable. We didn't say much on the ride up to Kansas City. I felt uncomfortable with the situation and it was incredibly awkward. When we got there though, and we were smack-dab in the middle of all the drunken debauchery, I instinctively kept Molly close to me, as close as possible without me putting my arm around her. I knew better than to make that mistake again! Being new to the community, she was spiritually weak, and I could tell she was struggling with the whole drunken scene. What I didn't realize at the time, but would later learn, is that this scene had been all too familiar to her, so most of her struggle was in being reminded of a past she was hoping to leave behind.

That summer, Eved and I were sent walking. We'd hitchhiked to Springfield. We walked all over that town, talking to people and handing out freepapers. We came across a young man who'd said he just read a paper online and he wondered if it was from us. He said it was called, "Rasta Dreams." Of course, I thought this was surely from God, that He wanted us to encounter this young man. It couldn't have been a coincidence that I was meeting him here in Missouri and he'd just read a paper I'd helped write while I was living in California. After talking to him for a while, he'd said he had to go, but that he might come visit the farm to see it for himself.

It was extremely hot and humid, and Eved and I had been walking for a while. We had emptied our water bottles and desperately needed more water. We ended up in front of the headquarter building for The Worldwide Church of God. I suggested we go inside and ask for some water. We were immediately greeted by several guards when we walked in, and they did not seem happy to see us. I told them that we were out preaching the gospel and we were just hoping to get some water, but they told us that there was no water. They directed us to a restaurant down the road that caters to homeless people once per week. It was about a seven or eight block walk away. I couldn't help but thinking about Matthew 25: 41-46.

Then He will also say to those on His left, 'Depart from Me, accursed ones, into the eternal fire which has been prepared for the devil and his angels;

for I was hungry, and you gave Me nothing to eat;

I was thirsty, and you gave Me nothing to drink;

I was a stranger, and you did not invite Me in; naked, and you did not clothe Me;

sick, and in prison, and you did not visit Me.'

Then they themselves also will answer, 'Lord, when did we see You hungry, or thirsty, or a stranger, or naked, or sick, or in prison, and did not take care of You?'

Then He will answer them, 'Truly I say to you, to the extent that you did not do it to one of the least of these, you did not do it to Me.'

These will go away into eternal punishment, but the righteous into eternal life.

We walked the seven or eight blocks to the restaurant, where there were already a few homeless people waiting for a meal. It would be about a two hour wait, but we would first need to hear a sermon in a large room attached to the restaurant. A couple arrived in a minivan. They had some musical instruments, which I helped them carry into the large room. We all gathered, Eved and I, along with all the homeless people. There were probably about 80 to 100 people in all. The man stood in front of everyone and started singing and playing guitar, while the woman played the keyboard. It was some sort of up-beat Christian song, and the woman looked all too pleased to be doing the Lord's work, in preaching to these homeless people and helping them with this one meal per week. She had such a smug, self-satisfied look on her face; it was nauseating. After several songs, the man started preaching and then opened up the floor for people to read their favorite bible verses that gave them daily comfort. After a few people stood up and spoke, I decided to do so as well. I read Deuteronomy 15:4.

However, there will be no poor among you, since the LORD will surely bless you in the land which the LORD your God is giving you as an inheritance to possess.

I told them, in front of all those homeless people, that they can't possibly know what this verse is supposed to mean, because they live in their comfy suburban home and come visit poor people once a week and feel really good about themselves for doing it. I explained how Eved and I came from a community where there truly were no poor among us, because we shared all things in common, as they did in the book of Acts, and everything was distributed to meet everyone's needs. I said that if anyone there wanted to join us, we'd feed them in the community, and we wouldn't just go our separate ways afterward. "We'll live in the same house as you! We'll even share a bunk with you!" Of course, they had some sort of rebuttal for me and at that point Eved stood up, grabbed his backpack and turned to me and said, "Let's go." So, I grabbed my backpack too, and we both walked out, without eating. A few people seemed shocked that we were leaving right then. They were just about to eat. Some of these homeless people couldn't imagine why we'd sit through this unbearable sermon, only to leave, right at the end, without eating. Eved and I weren't homeless though, so that was the difference. We didn't think it was right to have to listen to these people's lies just to get fed, and we didn't need to either.

We walked to the highway and started hitchhiking. We'd walked a good long while before anyone picked us up, and it was dangerously hot. At one point, I took out my water bottle and unscrewed the lid. I held it upside down to show the people in the passing cars, and I started screaming, "We need water!" We did get a ride to the town of Buffalo, and a janitor in a church was kind enough to let us in and fill up our bottles with water from the drinking fountain. We slept in the bushes that night. We had slept in the bushes the night before, too, in a park in Springfield. The next day, by the time we'd made it back to Weaubleau, the young man we'd met in Springfield had arrived at the farm.

Eved's wife came running out to greet him when we made it back. She leapt into his arms, gave him a good, long hug, and then took him back inside. Nobody had greeted me, and it felt really odd. It was like I didn't exist. It really sucked, being a single brother. When I went upstairs to the single brother's room, that's when I saw the young man from Springfield, talking to Ben Nabiy and Amittai, the two other single brothers who were living on the farm at that time. The young man had a ukulele, which was cool, and he played a few songs for us. He even taught me a few chords. He stayed a few days, but things went south when he'd decided to stop taking his medications, even though the leaders had advised otherwise. The young man started acting more and more crazy. At one point, I walked upstairs and saw him standing naked in the hallway. He shouted, "Look at me!" We had to get his grandmother to pick him up, and a few of the brothers grabbed him and forced him into her car, while he kicked and screamed that he didn't want to leave. It was really a disturbing thing to have witnessed, but I later found out that it had been especially devastating for Molly. She did not like the way the brothers had handled that situation and she took a long walk that day to try and sort out her thoughts about it.

I had been working with Naboth that year. He'd taken charge of the garden. We'd built two huge hoop houses and planted quite a beautiful garden, though we weren't half as good of a team as Yohanan Patman and I had been. Naboth was an elder and he knew it. He made it very clear by his commands that he was in charge and he did not seem the least bit welcoming to my opinions. Once, in the peak of the season, I'd asked him about possibly returning to the Bolivar farmer's markets, as I'd had a good experience when Yohanan and I had gone. Naboth was not interested in doing any markets. He gave no explanation, he just did not want us to participate in the farmer's markets, despite having plenty of produce we could have sold.

We did, however, go to the Wakarusa music festival that year. This time it was me, Naboth, and Eshet. Instead of sneaking in, we'd purchased booth space. Eshet had put together a few poster boards displaying a collage of photos from the farm. So, we just sat in this booth, talking to the few people who'd occasionally stop in. It was incredibly uncomfortable for me, sitting there with this older couple as young women would walk by wearing pasties over their boobs and little fox tails on their butts. I was both embarrassed at how other people would perceive me, like some young loser at this music festival with his grandparents, and embarrassed at watching these women that would normally have aroused me, while Naboth and Eshet were sitting right next to me. I wanted so badly to just be able to go have a fun time like all the other young people.

By this time, it had been a year since I'd seen Caitlin, so after we'd gotten back to the farm, I'd asked Naboth about her. I reminded him of my desire to go on a waiting period with her. It seemed to me like enough time had passed, and I really wanted to know what the leaders were thinking about it. He told me he'd bring it up in their next meeting. After the next meeting, I asked if they'd decided anything and he told me they hadn't talked about it. He said they had more important things to discuss. At this point, I was becoming quite fed-up with being lied to and I had thoroughly lost trust in my leaders. First it was, "Until the leaves change color" and now, one year later, they kept saying, "the next meeting." The massively tragic concealment of Rakefet's passing was also still fresh in my mind. It had been a horrible thing to do, to deceive people like that—to allow them to go on thinking she was still alive, knowing full-well she'd died. These leaders demanded that I trust them, yet they'd given me no reason to do so, other than the plethora of teachings that threatened eternal torment for anyone who distrusted authority. The teachings were no longer enough to convince me. What good was a threat of torment for disobedience, when I was already being tormented for my obedience?

I admired people who could live this communal life, people who believed not only in the lifestyle, but in the god who made it possible. I admired their sincerity and their genuine faith. Yet, there were only a few people in whom I was able to recognize such qualities. Elkanah had been one of those men, as had Tamiym, clinging to God and the anointing even through difficult personal struggles. Another such man was Othniel. Othniel had a son, about eight years old, and we lived together on the farm.

Othniel's son once fell from the second-floor loft in the farmhouse, as we were doing some construction work. I was walking towards the open door to the house when he fell, and it was one of the most horrifying things I'd ever witnessed. I could see him through the doorway and I watched helplessly as he fell face-first. I was too far away to have done anything. All I could do was throw my arms up in terror and run towards him. The boy was screaming and bleeding when I got to him. Fortunately, he only suffered a cut on the chin and a sprained arm. It could have been far more devastating. He could have broken several bones, or worse—he could have snapped his neck and been killed. What really struck me about the whole incident though was that before the boy had even hit the ground, his father, who was also watching helplessly, had screamed, "Abba, help us!" That was Othniel's first instinct—to scream for God to help his son. That, to me, exhibited an immense amount of sincerity, of legitimate faith—a level of faith that I have never possessed, nor will I ever be able to.

I continued to live in the community despite the constant inner turmoil. I found myself wanting to leave more than I wanted to stay, but I still didn't know where else I could go. This all changed when my sister invited me to her wedding in Northern Michigan. I mentioned it to a few people, not really expecting to be sent. Daveed had asked me if I wanted to go and I said I was indifferent about it. It just so happened though, that there was a woman at the farm who was also from Michigan. She had also been named Eshet, but she was much younger than Naboth's wife. She was married to a man named Yaqar, so we called her Eshet Yaqar and the other Eshet was Eshet Naboth. This was both to differentiate them and to signify who they belonged to. Yaqar and Eshet's wedding had been the first community wedding I'd seen, back in Colorado, all those years ago. Now they had two young daughters, and they were living on the farm. The leaders decided that Yaqar's family and I should drive up to Michigan together.

Seeing most of my family again was difficult. Some of them I hadn't seen in eight years, some even longer. My mother and sister were the only relatives I'd seen at all in the seven and a half years I'd lived in the community. Dan, my sister's father, was now dying from cancer. He was not the happy, energetic man I'd known before. Even so, he still had his farm, with so much potential, and I'd learned so

166

much about farming, so I thought maybe I'd be able to help him. I didn't say that, but it was a thought I had. He had allowed us to stay with him the weekend of the wedding. It was at that time that he'd said to me, "If you ever need a place to stay, don't hesitate to ask. I'm always here for you." It was something to think about.

At the wedding reception, I conveniently forgot I was a disciple from the Twelve Tribes. Yaqar and Eshet had gone to hand out free-papers and then went back to Dan's place when it got dark, so there was no one at the reception to judge me for acting like everybody else—like just a normal person from "the world." There was an open bar, and I'd drank a couple glasses of wine., not enough to get drunk, but certainly more than a true disciple would. There was also a cute girl serving the drinks, so I kind of flirted with her a little bit. My great uncle, who was seventy-something was also flirting with her. We left the next morning, drove back down-state, and stayed the night at Eshet's father's house.

Eshet's dad had put me in a guest bed, which was in his base-ment, while Yaqar and his family had a room upstairs. There were some drawers next to the bed, which I'd discovered were filled with porn magazines. Of course, I looked through each and every one of those magazines, as it had been quite a while since I'd seen anything like it. It was exciting at first, but it quickly got boring. I found myself longing to see a thicker woman than the women presented in those magazines. That was something else to think about. I realized by then that I was cut-off, but for the first time since joining the community, I'd also realized that I didn't care.

The next morning, Eshet's father decided to take his family to the Detroit zoo. I reconnected with my old friends, Charles the painter, and Ras Kente the musician. Charles and Ras Kente took me to a Thai restaurant in Ferndale, then to Ras Kente's place in Highland park. We spent the day together, talking about old times and watching BET. They'd told me they had gone to Belle Isle Park that morning, "looking for some pussy." It was at that point that I really began to see clearly how ridiculously exclusive the community had been. These guys weren't evil. They were just normal guys, but they, like everyone on Earth, were part of a specific culture. They would never have joined the community, because the community wasn't for them. Their culture and the community's culture would have been so at-odds with each other, that it would literally be impossible for such people to join the community. That's why there will never be a Twelve Tribes community in Detroit, or in any other predominantly black city, or in the entire continent of Africa.

The Twelve Tribes Communities were founded by a southern white man, the son of a preacher, who I suspect was likely involved with the KKK. Their teachings are too similar for there to not be any connection there. Even if neither Yonéq nor his father were directly involved with the Klan, they were certainly still influenced by the Klan, and were members of the same culture that had produced the Klan. Yohanan Abraham, the southern black man, who had become the Twelve Tribes' spokesman for the Cham teaching, had made it very clear by his glorification of the Klan, that the community had been influenced by the Klan's teachings. After all, how could one glorify something without it influencing them? The community had taught that the Holy Spirit had not walked the earth for 1900 years, until Yonéq came along, and yet the Twelve Tribes was spawned from a culture that dates back to the early days of the slave trade. I could see all of this so clearly now, and if the community was not for Charles and Ras Kente, then maybe it wasn't for me either. Maybe that's why I had always had such a hard time with fully giving myself to the community's beliefs, to the god of the Twelve Tribes.

I'd confessed everything to Yaqar—the wine and flirting at the reception, as well as the pornographic magazines at Eshet's father's house. I'm not a deceiver. I wasn't going to pretend like I was still connected when I wasn't. I spent the rest of my time in the community cut-off, never to be restored again. The realization I'd had about my own sexuality—that skinny women were boring to me and that I was really only attracted to thick women, had caused me to look at Molly differently than I had before. It's amazing, looking back now, how sheltering myself from the rest of the world in such a major way had affected me. I had completely forgotten who I was. I didn't even know who I was sexually attracted to, because I'd been surrounded by skinny women, and because I was forced to ignore my natural desires for such a long period of time. It was funny, Yaqar had given a teaching after our trip, and I was sitting across the room from Molly. The teaching was just more indoctrination about separating oneself from "the world," mentioning "worldly magazines," which is to say, any magazine published outside of the community. The community thought Cosmopolitan was evil, and I had just got done looking at pornos! I was sitting there during that teaching, listening, but also fantasizing about being with Molly. I could see the shape of her body, even through the modest clothing the community made her wear. It would be 110 degrees in the summer time in Missouri, and still the community would make the women wear such bulky clothes, because of how important modesty was to them.

The same teaching quotes 1 Peter 1:6-9, which was often quoted:

In this you greatly rejoice, though now for a little while, if need be, you have been grieved by various trials, that the genuineness of your faith,

being much more precious than gold that perishes, though it is tested by fire, may be found to praise, honor, and glory at the revelation of Jesus Christ (Yahshua), whom having not seen you love.

Though now you do not see Him, yet believing, you rejoice with joy

inexpressible and full of glory, receiving the end of your faith—the
salvation of your souls.

I was listening to the teaching go on about incorruptible faith, and comparing faith, which is eternal, to gold that will (according to the teaching) eventually erode, though after "a very long time." So, as incorruptible as gold is, our faith ought to be even more so. The thought that came to me was, "If faith really was incorruptible, then what harm would there be in looking at a magazine? Is your eternally, incorruptible faith going to be corrupted by a damn magazine?" From that time on, those were the types of thoughts that would come to me every time I'd hear a teaching, read a Bible verse, or listen to someone share in the gathering. From that time on, I questioned everything, and that is why I was never reconnected.

7

CONTROLLING MY OWN DESTINY

Despite not being connected, I continued to work hard. There was another WOOFer that came to join us on the farm: a man named Mike. He and I worked together a lot, fixing fences and helping build a pole barn that Naboth had decided we needed. We also stayed in the same room together, which at that time was an old, wooden trailer which was parked where the chicken coop used to be. The single brothers had to move out there to make more room in the house for families. I told Mike all about my struggles, about Caitlin, and he seemed to have nothing but sympathy for me. He was just a normal, hard-working man who also questioned things a lot when it came to religion. He'd often sit through the gatherings with his ball cap on, pulled down slightly over his eyes. He'd lean back in his seat, his feet stretched out in front of him, and his head down, looking like the tired farm hand he was. Mike's plan was to learn as much as he could about farming and then start his own farm at around the age of fifty. I found this plan to be somewhat depressing. I mean, fifty? I couldn't imagine working so long, without pay, and not being able to do my own thing until age fifty. I wasn't even so sure I'd live that long!

It was depressing for me to continue working without any motivation, and not getting payed for my work. I didn't know what I was living for anymore, but I enjoyed conversations. Mid-afternoon tea breaks with Mike became my favorite daily activity, and I'd sometimes take the opportunity to talk to Molly a little bit, as she would often be the only woman working in the kitchen. The women who had children would be putting their kids down for naps at that time of day. Molly had been cut-off shortly after I had, though I wasn't sure why. Seeing her struggle in the same way I was, I said to her once, "Well, it's better than a Turkish prison." Admittedly, I've never been to prison before, much less in Turkey, but it was probably still an accurate statement.

I'd often thought about women and how they'd become this possession, owned by the community. Women were given to certain men at the community's discretion. So, the fact that I was now a twenty-eight-year-old virgin had nothing to do with my personality or my physical appearance. It was simply the result of not having been deemed worthy enough by the community to be given a woman. I was at the prime of my life. I'd given the strength of my youth to the community. I'd grown food for them, taken care of their children, made money on various jobs for them, and none of it benefited me. I once thought I'd see my reward in the next age, after Yahshua returned, but I started to realize that this was not going to happen. I wanted to finally do something for myself, but I'd have to start life all over again, with nothing to my name, but a pair of shoes and a few articles of clothing—no money, no valuable possessions, not even a family of my own. I had nothing. I once laid on the floor in the trailer all day, contemplating these things. I was supposed to be working with Naboth, but he hadn't even checked on me once the whole day. That made it clear to me how little he cared.

During the week leading up to Yom Kippur, Jehu decided he wanted me to work with him. Jehu and Yaqar ran the community's cottage industry, which was a rustic furniture shop. They called it, "Ozark Rustic." At the time, Jehu was working on table tops for a large order they'd gotten, so he needed someone to help with the sanding, staining and urethane. It was easy work and it made room for some interesting, and at times even enlightening, conversations. The first conversation began on the ride up to the woodshop in Warsaw. Shomer was doing a job in the area at the time, so we'd gotten a ride with him. Being concerned for my current spiritual state, Shomer and Jehu turned their attention towards me. As much as I hated being the center of attention, being cut-off was a very public event, and people couldn't help but notice when you are not raising your hands or wearing your diadem in the gathering. People often want to help you, to encourage you to be restored in your faith. I was often encouraged to share what was going on with me, what was "in my heart." This was especially true for the week of Yom Kippur, when, according to the community's custom, people were supposed to be confessing their iniquities. This was something I'd participated in each year, but not this time. This time I was merely a spectator.

They'd asked me what I'd thought about what people had been sharing during that time, and I'd been brutally honest. I told them that some of what was said seemed fake. People who rarely said anything the rest of the year, much less with emotion, suddenly decided to "open-up" in front of everyone, simply because it was the thing to do at that time of year. I especially noticed it in Eshet Naboth, who was Shomer's mother, his "imma." She'd been almost as complacent as her husband the rest of the year and so to see her sad and emotional was odd, to say the least. But what was worse was that it almost seemed as if she was fake-crying. I'd lived with her for years. I knew the way she was. I'd even seen her be legitimately sad about stuff before, but this whole crying over her iniquities thing was different. It just seemed like a show—a public display. I mean, after all, you could confess stuff privately and be forgiven just as well, but during Yom Kippur people confessed stuff in the gatherings, in front of the whole community, and it almost seemed to turn into this contest of who could be more contrite in their repentance. Of course, Shomer didn't like the fact that I was saying these things about his imma. I wasn't trying to judge her. It was just the impression I'd gotten. They'd asked for my opinion and I'd given it. Shomer sternly warned me that I was "in a dangerous place."

What was more, it had gotten to the point that confessing stuff had become banal. I could predict what people were going to tell me based on my confession. There was a response for everything. It was always from a teaching, a bible verse, or a witty little phrase the community had invented, like, if someone was being proud about something, they'd say, "Pride comes before the fall." (A reference to Proverbs 16:18.) If you were being strongly opinionated, they'd say, "When you're strong, you're wrong.", or, "It's better to be wrong together than right alone." If you were struggling to believe in God, it was always Psalm 14:1 "The fool says in his heart, 'There is no God'." Then there were all the analogies—so many analogies! "Pick up your cross and die daily." "Be like sheep, not like goats." "The wheat stays, but the chaff is blown away." "Life is like a box of chocolates." Okay, maybe that last one wasn't from the community, but I'm sure I thought about it a lot during this time when I was getting sick of analogies.

Jehu told me that I was like the guy on the battlefield who has binoculars and stands back at a distance, telling all the people fighting in the battle what to do. He was referring to the night before, when I was sitting at the dinner table with Eshet Yaqar and her daughters.

Eshet was repeatedly giving the same command to one of her daughters and I'd said, "Discipline on the first command." It was one of those little phrases that the community used to death. In fact, it was the most used and most important instruction from the child training teachings. I'd said it, because I'd gotten sick of everybody's hypocrisy. They always had their eyes on me, because I'd been cut-off. They were constantly judging me, which was easy, because I was just a lowly single brother, but then they didn't do what their own teachings said to do. Eshet Yaqar was very offended by what I said, so she just got up and left. She went upstairs to her room, leaving me with her children until Yaqar finally came down to get them a while later.

The conversation really got interesting after Jehu and I got dropped off at the woodshop and we were alone all day. This went on for several days that week. He'd tell me stories about growing up in the back woods of West Virginia. His father had been a military man. Jehu's dad used to tell him things like, "Even a blind hog can find an ear of corn once in a while." Jehu was a tall, lanky man with dark hair and a southern drawl. He had an attractive wife, whom he'd married in his early days of living in the community. He'd joined the community when he was nineteen and now he was about forty. He was also in perfect health. Some of the things he'd told me kind of shocked me a little bit. For instance, he and his wife had developed a liking for the musical stylings of John Denver.

Now, typically the community was pretty closed-off when it came to music, or any cultural influences from the outside world. The rationale was that music comes from a spirit, and the Holy Spirit couldn't possibly live outside of the community, and yet, they accepted certain music as coming from "the righteous." They liked traditional Irish music and Appalachian mountain folk, because this type of music was invented by hard-working righteous folks. Of course, they didn't care much about the music that hard-working farmers in China listened to. The community loved to talk about the hard-working farmer in The Three Eternal Destinies. They didn't give a damn about Chinese culture, at least not their music, language or art. They did eat with chopsticks as a way to reach-out to "Yapheth" in hopes that if an Asian person visited a community, they would be impressed when they saw all the disciples eating with chopsticks, but given the fact that nothing from any Asian country's culture was even considered by the Twelve Tribes, them eating with chopsticks was just patronizing and ignorant. Of course, according to the community, there were also no righteous in Africa, so nothing from any African culture had been acknowledged by them either. It's a religion that very much glorifies southern culture and a few other white cultures, but nothing else. It had become abundantly clear to me that what was approved by the anointing was very much a matter of Yonéq's personal preference, and being a white southerner, it was no wonder that white and southern culture would be shown favoritism.

Jehu was a white southerner. The community's culture had been easy for him to accept. That isn't to say that life in the community was easy for anybody. It was still a life of servitude, of working for other people without any expectation of personal gain, but how one perceived the community is very much connected to where they are coming from. And being that it was easier to live a life of servitude when one actually believed in what they were doing, I felt like it was easier for Jehu than it was for me. He couldn't relate to me. He had no idea why I'd been having such a hard time, and he saw it as weakness. Even so, I loved the conversations, and I found them to be thoroughly stimulating, intellectually.

Jehu talked about how people were in control of their own destiny. He said he didn't know why people talked about not being able to get out of the ghetto. "It's easy to get out of the ghetto," he'd said. "You just leave. Just go somewhere else. Get a job at a gas station if you have to. This is America. It's the easiest country in the world to find a job and pursue your dreams." He told me a story about a man he knew that had escaped a war-torn country in Eastern Europe. He said that the man swam across a river as guards with machine guns were shooting at him. There were other men getting shot and dying on either side of this man, but somehow, this friend of Jehu's had made it across the river alive, and had escaped to freedom. "If you don't like the way things are in the community," he told me, "just do something about it."

He told me a story about his time at the farm in Hillsboro. He said they needed a fence, so he just started building it. None of the leaders knew which one of them had ordered Jehu to build the fence, but each one assumed that one of them had. Before long, the leaders started having other men help Jehu and they helped him get supplies, and the fence had been built in no time. This had been hard for me to hear because throughout my whole time in the community, I'd heard so many teachings about "lawlessness," which was what the community called doing anything you weren't sent to do, and I'd been directly told, so many times, that you don't do anything without being sent. Yet, Jehu seemed to be perfectly comfortable doing what had to be done, even if it was just something that he thought needed to be done, and not something the brothers had decided in council. I guess I'd been doing it all wrong the whole time! It would have been much easier for me if I could have had Jehu's attitude and ignored what the teachings said, just did whatever work I thought needed to be done, and listen to whatever worldly music I wanted to listen to, and go on thinking I have faith, and judging others for not having faith. That would have been so much easier for me! But that wasn't me. Maybe that worked for Jehu, but it wasn't going to cut it for me.

I asked him, "If I can do anything I want to, why can't I just go talk to a single sister then?" He laughed and said, "Who would you talk to, Molly?" He'd said it like it was a joke. He'd been so condescending about it, like it was ridiculous that anybody would be attracted to her. Jehu was accustomed to those small community girls, but to each his own. He had no idea that I had started taking a liking to Molly, and I preferred to keep it that way. It was all so clear now. Everything was just personal preference and subjective opinions, but I wasn't going to keep allowing my life to be dictated by another man's personal preference.

My experiences were different than Jehu's, and that's why I thought differently than he did. I saw the world through different eyes. I didn't believe that a person could determine their own destiny—not entirely. I didn't choose to be born with sickle cell, yet it has had such a profound influence on my life, in many cases determining my circumstances, causing not only pain, but at times, even financial hardships. The slaves in the south didn't choose to be born black, yet being born black had determined their circumstances for the rest of their lives. Those are the types of things that a person born healthy, white, and free, could never possibly relate to, and so yes, for them, their circumstances would be largely determined by their actions, and they would be very much in control of their own destiny— just as someone born rich would have more control of their destiny than someone born into poverty. Sure, a slave could escape, but they would be hunted down like a dog. The men who'd tried to escape that Eastern European country alongside of Jehu's friend were in control of their own destiny, until they got shot.

I now believe that life is often what you make it, and I do my best to maintain a positive attitude about things, to always look on the bright side, but I'm also in reality. I know when my circumstances have gotten the better of me. It's not an either-or type of thing. It's not complete control of your destiny, or none. You make do with what you have, strive for a better life, and accept that shit's going to happen anyway, no matter what you do.

I did take control of my own destiny. When the rest of the community was having breaking of bread, Molly and I were left out. It was the perfect opportunity for me to approach her. She told me she wanted to leave, and she was thinking about hitchhiking. That's when I asked her to meet me at the trailer. I wasn't sure if she'd show up, and I was pretty nervous. I wasn't even sure if she liked me at that time, so I was making a pretty big gamble. Mike was out there with me, and I'd told him what was going on. He really liked Molly. Unlike the other women, who were always so serious and judgmental, Molly had always been friendly to the both of us. She came to the door, and she and I went for a walk together, out by the orchard and the goat barn, away from the houses. I told her about Dan, and about the farm. It was the only place I knew of that I could go back to. She'd thought about it, and the next day she'd given me a note. I still have the note. I keep it in my wallet.

Lev Rak,

I thought I could more easily write down the things I want to say. So far, my time in the community has been very beneficial to me by building a better character than the one I got growing up. All the things I have heard about controlling your reactions and the respect women have for men, are truly wonderful things that the whole world should know and they are things that I want to take with me wherever I go. I think I really do want to leave this place and I feel like I am willing to go anywhere so long as I am not alone. I appreciate how respectful you are. It is something pretty rare, and I am not really used to it. I'm sure it's crossed your mind, but one of my greatest hindrances is what other people think about my skin. You seem so genuinely nice, that I sense it is not the problem I think it is. I'm sure there is more I could say if I were in the right place, but basically, what I am saying is that I feel I don't have anything left to lose and I am willing to go with you wherever you would want to go.

Let me know what you think,

Molly

I really hadn't noticed anything odd about her skin. That had been the only confusing thing about the letter. I'd asked her about it, and she said she had psoriasis. She was right though, that it wasn't a problem for me. She just looked like she had more reddish skin than most people, but I'm not too concerned about skin color. The important thing was that she was actually willing to go with me. I can't accurately describe how it made me feel at the time. I was excited and scared. Everything was about to change.

I went on a job with Ben Nabiy that day. He was an experienced plumber, so he was finishing up the job Shomer had started, building a house for someone out in the woods, between Warsaw and Weaubleau. I'd heard some news that same day about my friend Tamiym, from Warsaw. Apparently, he'd showed up to a job completely drunk. He was fired by the foreman, and had brought shame to the community. So, they sent him away, which was the community's polite way of saying he got kicked out.

Ben Nabiy's religiousness was obnoxious. He had an arrogant, "me and Jesus have a good thing going," type of attitude. He may have been an experienced plumber, but he was relatively new to the community. He too had tried to get me to repent and be reconnected, but I wasn't having it. He'd told me how focused he was on being humble, which was probably his failed attempt at getting me to humble myself too. He thought he was leading by example. He certainly wasn't expecting me to respond to him the way I did. I'd said, "How can you be humble when you're so focused on yourself? That seems kind of proud to me. I mean, trying to make yourself humble?" I felt like if the most important thing for somebody, their primary focus, is that they themselves are humble, then they're kind of missing the point. I mean, everything else we did in the community was for others, so what was all this self-improvement bullshit all about? To be humble, so you can be saved? So what? So you can go to Heaven? To me, being humble was about listening to others. It was about giving up my strong opinions as I'd done so many times in the past. It was about the ability to get along with other people, to love them, and to forget about yourself. It wasn't about me. It was about building the kingdom. At least, that's what it had always been about for me before. That's why I'd felt so guilty about all the times I wasn't doing those things. That's why I'd always confessed my sins, even when no one else would have known what I'd done. I needed to be absolved of the guilt, so I could continue to function as a disciple and build the kingdom, not so I could go to Heaven and avoid Hell.

None of that mattered any more, though. I was no longer under a delusion that I was building some sort of divine kingdom on Earth. I just didn't want to listen to this guy talk to me about how humble he was. I'd told him about Molly, and I'd even showed him the note. He'd seemed pretty flustered by my response to him about being humble, and he even seemed to be getting kind of angry. Later that evening, he shared in the gathering about the birds pecking out children's eyes if they disrespect their parents (Proverbs 30:17). This was how Ben Nabiy viewed his relationship with God. It was always about doing good so you'll be rewarded, and not punished. He'd focused on these threats—threats of eternal damnation, or of getting your eyes pecked out. He went on preaching about this in such an intense way that some of us became very disturbed by it. It had especially affected Mike. So, after the gathering, Mike complained about Ben Nabiy to some of the brothers, calling it child abuse, since he was clearly instilling an unhealthy amount of fear into those innocent kids. At the same time, Ben Nabiy complained to some of the brothers about me, and he told them about the note Molly had given me.

Later that night, Molly and I got called into a meeting. Naboth, Daveed, Othniel, and Yaqar were all there. A lot was said, but by the end of the meeting, it was made clear that Molly and I would not be allowed to stay in the community, and we were both okay with that. They'd offered to buy us a bus ticket and asked where we wanted to go. I said, "Traverse City, Michigan." Othniel gave us a dire warning, but it came out kind of funny. At least I thought it was a little funny-sounding. He'd said, "No matter how bad or not bad you think it's going to be, it will be worse." I didn't laugh, but I just thought it was kind of a funny threat. Anyway, I didn't expect it to be easy, starting over in the world with nothing to my name. If I thought it was going to be easy, I'd have left much sooner. The real threat was what the community constantly taught us, regardless of whether we were considering leaving or not. They'd always told us that if we left the community, we were rejecting the true gospel, and if we rejected the true gospel, we would spend eternity in the lake of fire.

By this time, I'd begun to have a very cynical perspective on the concept of eternal damnation. It probably stemmed from being controlled for so many years. Every aspect of my life was not only subjected to criticism, but it was also dictated. I could do nothing independently. If I did, I'd risk eternity in the lake of fire. This got me thinking: If I were to start my own religion, and I had to think of the greatest incentive I could possibly think of to convert and control the gullible masses, what incentive would I come up with? Well, I could try to tell people that their lives are worthless without my religion, and indeed the community did this. I could tell people that my religion would give them fulfillment and purpose. The community did this too. But what's an even greater incentive? *Think big. Think: Eternity!* What if you told people that if they joined your religion, they would experience an eternity of bliss, but if they *didn't* join your religion, they'd be tormented for eternity? Before long, you'd have people asking themselves, "What if he's right? What if I'm wrong? If I believe in his religion, and I'm wrong, then nothing happens, but if I *don't* believe in his religion and I'm wrong, I'll be tormented for eternity. That would be the worst thing ever! Okay, I'll join his religion, and if he's right, I'll have an eternity of bliss." I couldn't think of a greater incentive than the promise of eternal bliss and the threat of eternal torment. It was almost as if somebody sat down and thought this stuff up and came up with Christianity, and of course, Islam followed, and now we have many thousands of variations of both Christianity and Islam. It was almost as if it was by design! I thought, *Is it coincidence that some of the world's most successful religions use this incentive to gain converts?*

After the meeting, I went back out to the trailer. I let Mike know what was going on, packed my bags, and then we said our good-byes. Daveed had gotten us a bus ticket, and he gave us a ride to Des Moines. It had been a long ride, late at night. He dropped us off right around dawn, and he gave me a phone card that had about ten minutes left on it. I called Dan and let him know what was going on. He said he'd pick us up when we get to Traverse City. Molly and I waited a few hours for the bus to arrive. President Obama was on the television. They were playing his victory speech from his 2012 re-election, which had just taken place the night before. The president spoke about equality for all. He not only mentioned equality for people of different races, but also for people of different ages, income levels, physical abilities, and sexual orientations.

"I believe that we can keep the promise of our founding—the idea that if you're willing to work hard,

it doesn't matter who you are, or where you come from, or what you look like, or where you love.

It doesn't matter whether you're black or white, or Hispanic or Asian, or Native American, or young, or old,

Or rich or poor, abled, disabled, gay or straight. You can make it here in America, if you're willing to try."

We were immigrants. We were leaving one nation—the nation of New Israel, the Twelve Tribes, a nation in which women must be submissive to men, blacks and whites are not equal, homosexuality is a sin for which gays must repent if they want to be accepted, a nation where even differing beliefs and opinions are not allowed, where your daily activities are strictly dictated; and we were entering what is arguably the freest nation on the planet.

It was a long bus ride, but we were happy. Molly and I were eager to get to know each other, and excited to be facing our future together. We had a long wait when we arrived in Traverse City, too. I'd called Dan again and he'd said he was just leaving his house in Central Lake, so it'd be about an hour. We walked down to the park, out on the docks overlooking the Grand Traverse Bay. It was mostly empty, being a cold day in November. That's where we had our first kiss. It was my first kiss ever.

As I'd suspected, it hadn't been easy, trying to integrate back into the greater society. It had been a long, harsh winter on the farm. Dan wasn't his usual happy self. He was dying of cancer. There was a lot of pressure on Molly and me to find work, but Dan's farm was out in the woods, and it was about a five-mile hike in either direction to get to the towns of either Central Lake, or Bellaire. All the snow and ice certainly didn't help the hike, and we didn't always have access to a vehicle. I'd walk for miles to shovel people's driveways for just a little bit of cash. I didn't find full-time work until the following spring.

I got a job at a local organic farm, one of the biggest in the area. I was also growing a large market garden on Dan's farm. Molly and I found our own place to live. A charitable Christian family had offered us exceptionally cheap rent for a decent-sized home. We'd gotten married at the courthouse and we would have a baby that fall. I took a second job at a grocery store, working nights, stocking shelves. I'd work from 10pm, sometimes starting even as early as 8pm, until 7am the next morning, then I'd drive to the farm and harvest produce until noon.

The first time I saw our son on the ultrasound, the name 'Terrence' popped into my head. He just looked like a Terrence. I'd looked up the meaning of the name afterwards, and it means tender. We gave him the middle name Quin, which means wisdom. Quin was also my father's last name, so it should have been my last name too, but being raised by my mother, I was given her name instead. I felt it was fitting that my son would have the name Quin, and I liked how tender wisdom went together, like having knowledge with compassion. You can't just be a know-it-all, you have to care about people too. I'd heard it said that, "No one cares what you know, unless they know that you care." That was how I wanted my son to be—wise and knowledgeable, tender and compassionate.

When I first held my son, he was so small and fragile. He was vulnerable, entirely dependent, and innocent. I didn't want anything bad to ever happen to him. I thought to myself, *I know that there are bound to be hardships in life, and that these hardships build character, but I don't want my son to ever have to suffer needlessly. I want him to always be safe, warm, well-fed, and well cared for. I want him to be secure and to always know that he is loved—just as every child should. I don't want to spoil him. I want him to learn self-control and discipline, but at the same time, I never want anything bad to happen to him.* Terrence had been the cutest baby that ever lived. Now, he's not so cute anymore, but I love him just the same.

After a few years, I had to quit my physically demanding jobs. I kept having sickle cell crises. Molly went to work at a few different places, including the grocery store I'd worked at, giving me the opportunity to go back to school. I got a bookkeeping certificate, and ten days later I was hired as an administrative assistant at a warehouse.

During all this time, Molly and I both struggled to be "deprogrammed" from our conditioning in the community. I'd been there the longest, but I had already been questioning things quite a bit. Now, Molly and I have equality in our marriage. I do not see her as the weaker vessel, as the community taught. We are a partnership, and I am certainly not her boss. We love and respect each other very much, and we do the best we can. As I began to view life differently, I went from merely "questioning things" to the realization that religion is a lie and the god of the Bible simply does not exist. There are three main categories of thought that led me to arrive at this conclusion:

Culture, racism, and personal preference (in my mind, these are all part of the same category).

The size of the universe.

Religion versus morality.

8

CULTURE, RACISM, AND PERSONAL PREFERENCE

And the Lord said to Moses, "Go, get down! For your people whom you brought out of the land of Egypt have corrupted them-selves. They have turned aside quickly out of the way which I commanded them.

They have made themselves a molded calf, and worshiped it and sacrificed to it, and said, 'This is your god, O Israel, that brought you out of the land of Egypt!'"

And the Lord said to Moses, "I have seen this people, and indeed it is a stiff-necked people! Now therefore, let Me alone, that My wrath may burn hot against them and I may consume them.

And I will make of you a great nation."

Then Moses pleaded with the Lord his God, and said: "Lord, why does Your wrath burn hot against Your people whom You have brought out of the land of Egypt with great power and with a mighty hand?

Why should the Egyptians speak, and say, 'He brought them out to harm them, to kill them in the mountains, and to consume them from the face of the earth?'

Turn from Your fierce wrath, and relent from this harm to Your people.

Remember Abraham, Isaac, and Israel, Your servants, to whom You swore by Your own self, and said to them,

'I will multiply your descendants as the stars of heaven; and all this land that I have spoken of I give to your descendants, and they shall inherit it forever.'"

So the Lord relented from the harm which He said He would do to His people.

And Moses turned and went down from the mountain, and the two tablets of the Testimony were in his hand.

The tablets were written on both sides; on the one side and on the other they were written. Now the tablets were the work of God, and the writing was the writing of God engraved on the tablets.

(Exodus 32:7-16)

According to this story, the Israelites have Moses to thank for not having been destroyed by God, and for being made into a mighty nation instead. What I'd like to know is, who wrote this story? Early

Christian and Jewish tradition held that the first five books of the Bible were written by Moses himself.[7] [8] If this were true, then some portions of these scriptures would have been rather anomalous and difficult to explain. Take Numbers 12:3, for instance:

Now the man Moses was very humble, more than all men who were on the face of the earth.

If Moses had written these books himself, then much of these books are autobiographical. In modern times, if someone is going to make fantastical claims, such as being able to turn a stick into a snake, part the waters of a sea, or speak to a burning bush, people would want some sort of evidence to back up such claims. They'd want to hear from eye-witnesses, or see the video or photos before taking someone's word for it. That's just the world we live in today.

So, in this autobiographical story of Moses, he comes down from this mountain and says, "God wanted to kill you all, but I got Him to change His mind. You're welcome." This would have been a great way for somebody to assert their leadership over a superstitious people, but in reality, were there even any people there with him? Did he actually climb a mountain, or was this just some story he wrote? The truth is that today we simply do not know. We have no way of knowing what actually took place at that time, and there are no objective writings, written by others who witnessed these events. We have no writings from that time, because at that time, the Israelites were illiterate.

Most modern biblical scholars believe that the first five books of the Bible, also known as the Torah, were not written by Moses, but rather, they were written sometime during the Babylonian Captivity (from around 600 BC to 538 BC).[9] This theory is equally problematic, because if it's true it means that the Hebrew people, when writing down the stories in the Torah, would have had nothing to go off of except for oral history. Moses is believed to have died sometime between the 15th or 13th centuries BC,[10] [11] which would mean that about 600-800 years had passed before his story was finally written down.

Now, I would love to learn the truth of the matter, even if that truth contradicts my presently-held beliefs, but I am not naïve. Not anymore. I'm not going to live (the rest of) my life based on something that is possibly true, yet highly improbable. It's extremely unlikely that an accurate record of anything could be kept for several centuries by word-of-mouth.

However improbable this story may be, it has greatly impacted modern society, especially western cultures, in a very real way. So, I'll continue with the story: Shortly after Moses pleaded with God to spare his people, they did become a mighty nation, cutting off the toes and thumbs of enemy kings, making them crawl like dogs and eat scraps off the ground.[12] Through killing and enslaving, they quickly subdued the nations, not only from among the land they were to "inherit" from their god, but also the neighboring nations of what would become Israel. The killing of these nations had been a command from their god:

> *But of the cities of these peoples which the Lord your God gives you as an inheritance, you shall let nothing that breathes remain alive,*
>
> *but you shall utterly destroy them: the Hittite and the Amorite and the Canaanite and the Perizzite and the Hivite and the Jebusite,*
>
> *just as the Lord your God has commanded you,*
>
> *lest they teach you to do according to all their abominations which they have done for their gods, and you sin against the Lord your God.* (Deuteronomy 20:16-18)

It is important to note that many modern Christians sincerely believe that the nations mentioned in this passage were completely corrupt, practicing horrible, unspeakable crimes against humanity. They do not believe in a god that punished innocent people. They believe in a god that punished sin. This is a fair distinction to make, but it doesn't change what happened for the rest of human history, with these genocidal tendencies being passed on through the holy scriptures. The Hebrew people believed that they were the superior race, chosen by God, and that all other races were corrupt, cursed, and should be "utterly destroyed." This same attitude of racial superiority would eventually be adopted by European Christians and would become the fuel behind European Imperialism.[13]

The same god that commanded the Hebrew people to "utterly destroy" their neighbors and enslave the descendants of Cham, led the Europeans to commit genocide against indigenous peoples in the Americas[14 15], Africa[16 17], Asia[18], and even as far as Australia[19]. It was the same god that created the slave trade and preserved it through the use of the holy scriptures. Of course, this was not God, the creator of all humanity. This was man-made religion, and specifically, the religions which were based on the Bible. The history of European imperialism is sick, twisted and at times, ironic. It is a story of pride, nationalism, arrogance and ignorance. Ironically, Christianity, including Catholicism, was rife with anti-Semitism throughout the medieval period, despite the fact that it was the Hebrew people who had invented their religion.

In the year 374, Saint Ambrose of Milan had this to say about Jews:

"The Jews are the most worthless of all men. They are lecherous, greedy, rapacious. They are perfidious murderers of Christ.

They worship the Devil. Their religion is a sickness. The Jews are the odious assassins of Christ and for killing God there is no expiation possible, no indulgence or pardon.

Christians may never cease vengeance, and the Jew must live in servitude forever. God always hated the Jews. It is essential that all Christians hate them." [20]

A few years later, Saint John Chrysostom, bishop of Antioch said:

"Where Christ-killers gather, the cross is ridiculed, God blasphemed, the father unacknowledged, the son insulted, the grace of the Spirit rejected...If the Jewish rites are holy and venerable, our way of life must be false. But if our way is true, as indeed it is, theirs is fraudulent. I am not speaking of the Scriptures. Far from it!... I am speaking of their present impiety and madness." [21]

To this day, the Catholic church believes the men who said these things to be saints, chosen by God Himself. This is what the modern Catholic church has to say about their anti-Semitic saints:

"He [Saint Ambrose] was one of the most illustrious Fathers and Doctors of the Church, and fitly chosen, together with St. Augustine, St. John Chrysostom, and St. Athanasius, to uphold the venerable Chair of the Prince of the Apostles in the tribune of St. Peter's at Rome." [22]

England expelled all Jews in 1290[23], exactly 100 years after the infamous massacre of the Jews at York[24]. Another massacre, of thousands of Jews, occurred in Germany in 1298[25], and in 1306, Jews were expelled from France.[26] In 1483, expulsions took place from Warsaw,

Sicily, Lithuania, and Portugal.[27] In 1492, the same year Spain sent Christopher Columbus to the Americas, the Spanish monarchy also ordered the expulsion of the Jews from their country.[28] This followed the conversion of King Ferdinand and Queen Isabella to Catholicism, which also sparked the Spanish Inquisitions.[29] (Interesting side note: The Muslims had been tolerant of other religions, including Judaism, during their occupation of Spain[30], despite having been called by Pope Urban II, "an accursed race, a race wholly alienated from God.")[31] In 1569, Pope Pius V ordered all Jews out of the Papal states.[32] In 1593, the Jews were expelled from Italy and Bavaria.[33]

In 1715, Pope Pius VI issued an edict against Jews[34], and his reasoning was telling of what had led the Church to assume such a horrific, anti-Semitic stance in the first place:

> *"Among the pastoral solicitudes that occupy the soul of the Holiness of our Lord [i.e., the Pope] at the outset of his Pontificate,*
>
> *the foremost priority is that which guards the Catholic religion from corruption among the Faithful.*
>
> *Considering, therefore, the need to protect the faithful from the danger of subversion that can result from excessive familiarity with the Jews,*
>
> *the exact observance of the measures taken by [the Pope's] glorious predecessors is absolutely necessary."*[35]

The Catholic Church was attempting to preserve their dead,

godless religion by any means necessary. Having no real power given to them by God, Catholics, and virtually all medieval Christians, had to take matters into their own hands, using violence to preserve their religion. Their god couldn't protect them from so-called "corruption," so they had to separate themselves from the corrupters, the Jews, by killing them or by banning them from their countries. This is the same reason the Twelve Tribes Communities are so strict about limiting all influence from the outside world, and why they deceived us about Rakefet's death. It was all to preserve a dead religion and maintain their power over the people.

The Bible being an invention of the Hebrew culture is an important distinction to make. European culture had nothing to do with it. Yet, they "Europeanized" it, making it apply to their culture in unnatural ways. Just one example of this is the name of the savior, which was supposed to have been a Hebrew name (unless you actually believe that the angel Gabriel was speaking 17th century English when he came to Miriam, the savior's Hebrew mother). Rather than opting to use the name "Joshua" (which would have been more authentic), or its Hebrew version (which would be either Yehoshua, Yeshua, or Yahshua[36])[37], the translators changed each rendering of the savior's name to Jesus (the J was added after 1638, as evidenced by the fact that if you look at an English version Bible prior to 1638, you will see the name Iesus, but subsequent versions use the name Jesus). The name Jesus is based on the Greek word, "Iesous."[38] So, the name "Jesus" is the English variant of a Greek word. Also, the Greek, "Christos," meaning anointed, became "Christ."[39]

In my opinion, and as the Twelve Tribes believed, this change was probably made to avoid acknowledging the savior's Hebrew name, or at least to create a new, more Anglican-sounding name that would appeal to the English masses of the 17th Century. All of this is very disturbing to me. If He was a real person, then why change His name? And if He wasn't a real person, why lie to people and say He was?

The result of this name changing based on Greek words is that many people today believe that "Jesus Christ" is a real name. This is a misconception that only common folk have, not religious scholars, but it's still wide-spread, leading to more than a billion people praying to this made-up name. This worshipping of a savior whose name was an English variant of two Greek words was likely instrumental in allowing Christian Europeans to distance themselves from the Jews, who'd created their religion in the first place. The translators fucked up though, and the evidence of their anti-Semitic tampering can still be found in none other than the book of Hebrews:

For if Jesus had given them rest, then would he not afterward have spoken of another day. (Hebrews 4:8, King James version)

For if Joshua had given them rest, then He would not afterward

have spoken of another day. (Hebrews 4:8, virtually every other
English version)

So why does the King James version (after 1638) say "Jesus" in this verse, while virtually every subsequent English version, including the New King James, says Joshua? Simply put, the original translators were concerned primarily with language, while subsequent translators considered the context. The translators of the more recent versions realized that this verse, as well as Acts 7:45, was referring to Joshua of old, and not Jesus, whose real name (if He was a real person) was probably the Hebrew version of the name Joshua. The Greek word, Iesous, was the closest thing to the Hebrew, Yeshua or Yehoshua, which means "mighty and powerful to save." So, it would make sense that the Greek authors used this word "Iesous" when referring to the savior. It's a word. It means something. There's quite a bit of significance to the word, "Iesous." In fact, Philo of Alexandria even referred to it as "the most excellent of names." [40] So even as early as the 1st Century AD, this was a name that had significance and made sense as a transliteration. It makes no sense, however, to change the savior's name to "Jesus" every time it appears in the New Testament. Yet, that is precisely what the translators did, even when it was referring to Joshua of old.

Here's a little background: There were several translators of the original King James Bible (about sixty, depending on how you define the word "translator," because not all who worked on the KJV were expert linguists, directly involved with translating). All were men. Most were very well-educated, for their time, and they were all born into the same, specific culture: 16th century England.[41] Of course, we cannot know exactly what they were thinking when they did this, but I would imagine that, being proud Englishmen, they favored English culture over all others, including the Hebrew culture that invented their religion! They could just as easily have kept the savior's original Hebrew name, either Yeshua or Yehoshua, but they opted for the more English-sounding version. This was all due to personal preference, cultural pride, and perhaps a little (or a lot of) racism.

I sincerely wanted to know what was motivating these men, so I did quite a bit of research on the subject. In my searching, I did not find anything alluding to their motives, but I did find some rather amusing articles written by biblical apologists attempting to describe the KJV translators as "a diverse group." This assertion of diversity is, of course, based on the fact that, "some were from cities, and some from small villages." Also, some had been farmers and some had been teachers. So, even though each and every one of these translators was a white man from England, and a member of the Church of England, we're expected to believe that they were "a diverse group," because of the size of the towns they were from, or their previous employment? In my humble opinion, one's place of employment has little to do with one's broader cultural identity. These men had the great responsibility of accurately presenting 17th century England (it was the early 17th century by the time they began working on the KJV)[42] with an interpretation of a story from Hebrew culture prior to the first century. In this context, is it really a fair assessment to claim they were a diverse group?

Not surprisingly, the Church of England did not have a favorable opinion of the Jews at this time. England had expelled the Jews centuries before, and those who were around in the 16th and 17th centuries were not permitted to practice their faith openly.[43] So, I think it's safe to say that preserving Hebrew culture was not a top priority of the KJV translators. The Church of England also taught, during this time, that slavery was ordained by God.[44] In 2006, they officially apologized for their involvement in slavery.[45]

The concept of slavery based on race can be traced back to Genesis 9:18-26. If we are to believe that all humanity has descended from Noah and his sons, then this was the beginning of race-based involuntary servitude. These are the verses that led Christians to believe that race-based slavery had been ordained by God. All descendants of Canaan (the entire race of the Canaanites) were to be slaves to the descendants of Shem (called Shemites, which is where the word "Semite" comes from). Europeans took this doctrine a step further, believing that every non-Christian and non-European (thus indigenous peoples all over the globe) ought to be slaves to Christian Europeans, because that is how God intended it to be. This was once a commonly accepted doctrine within mainstream Christianity.[46] It wasn't just a product of the KKK and the Twelve Tribes Communities. However, the major Christian denominations changed their pro-slavery, anti-Semitic doctrines as popular public opinion on these matters began to shift.

I'm thankful that mainstream Christianity changed their doctrine on slavery, anti-Semitism, and racism in general. The world is a better place because of this change, but the real key here is that they changed their doctrine. Christians would like us to think that this paradigm shift was due to some sort of "moral awakening," but let's be clear here: The doctrine might have changed, but their objectives haven't. Rampant anti-Semitism was led by a desire to preserve the Christian religion, and this is the same objective that leads religions to change their doctrines. The ones who don't change over time to become more acceptable in the eyes of the general public will either die-out or become a fringe group, such as the KKK and the Twelve Tribes Communities. This is a basic principle of evolution: A species, or in this case a religion, that is best-suited to adapt, will be best-suited for survival. [47] That is why mainstream Christianity will eventually sanction homosexuality, the use of contraception, premarital sex, ecumenicalism, and everything else that appeals to popular culture. In my opinion, these are all good things, and such tolerance will promote personal freedom and limit prejudices. So, while I'm happy for this shift from the old, restrictive religion to a new, more open one, it's hardly proof of the religion's legitimacy.

All of this leads me to believe that religion is merely a product of personal preference and was not established by an all-powerful god. If it had been established by God Himself, there'd be no need to change it, as it would have been infallible. When you accept this view, reading Leviticus makes a lot more sense. It seems pretty clear that the book was written by a grossed-out man who had a bad experience with a menstruating woman and some old pork chops. The entire Levitical law is the result of personal preference. There is no way that the god who created the entire universe is going to be that obsessed with semen, menstruation, and which animals we can and cannot eat.

Considering Levitical law brings up another curious issue: Why don't modern Christians obey these laws? On the subject of unclean meat, Christians like to point out that Jesus said, "There is nothing that enters a man from outside which can defile him; but the things which come out of him, those are the things that defile a man" (Mark 7:15). This quote is also referenced, in a slightly different way, in Matthew 15:16-20, but Mark's version of the quote is more concise. Ironically, this quote is usually taken out of context. (I say ironically, because it has been my experience that Christians don't like it when people take Bible verses out of context.)

Here's how Matthew, chapter 15 begins:

*Then the scribes and Pharisees who were from Jerusalem came to Jesus, saying, "Why do Your disciples transgress the tradition of the elders? For they do not **wash their hands** when they eat bread."*

And here's how Mark, chapter seven begins:

*Then the Pharisees and some of the scribes came together to Him, having come from Jerusalem. Now when they saw some of His disciples eat bread with defiled, that is, with **unwashed hands**, they found fault. For the Pharisees and all the Jews do not eat unless they **wash their hands** in a special way, holding the tradition of the elders. When they come from the marketplace, **they do not eat unless they wash**. And there are many other things which they have received and hold, like the washing of cups, pitchers, copper vessels, and couches.*

*Then the Pharisees and scribes asked Him, "Why do Your disciples not walk according to the tradition of the elders, but eat bread with **unwashed hands?**"*

It wasn't a discussion on unclean meat that led Jesus to respond the way he did, saying that it isn't what goes into a man that makes him unclean. It was a discussion on ritualistic hand-washing that led him to say that. Jesus would not have eaten unclean meat, because He was a Jew. He wasn't permitting His followers to eat unclean meat either. He was justifying their actions to not engage in ritualistic hand-washing along with the Pharisees. If you take this quote as justification to eat bacon, then by that reasoning, you could just as easily take it as justification to have gay butt sex, because "There is nothing that enters a man from outside which can defile him."

Of course, whether you eat bacon or engage in gay sex, it's all a matter of personal preference, and I personally wouldn't judge anyone for that. For the Hebrew people, however, the law wasn't about personal preference. They sincerely believed, as many Jews do today, that the reason God gave them these laws was because they were chosen, out of all peoples on the face of the earth, to be his treasured possession, as it says in Deuteronomy 14:2 (NIV).

For you are a people holy to the LORD your God. Out of all the peoples on the face of the earth, the LORD has chosen you to be his treasured possession.

I would argue that even this is a matter of personal preference, and not the word of God. After all, was it not written by a Hebrew man? Would he not have given preference to his own culture? Should it surprise us, coming from a Hebrew man, that God, or rather his god, had chosen his culture, out of all other cultures on earth? If this had been written by a Canaanite, I might be more impressed. It might have been more convincing if Canaan had taught his descendants that they were to be the slaves of the descendants of Shem, but it didn't come from Canaan or his descendants. It came from Shem's descendants (the ones who were to be served, not the ones who were to be servants). This claim that God chose the Hebrew people, out of all other peoples on the face of the earth, didn't come from all other peoples on the face of the earth. That would have been really impressive! It came from the Hebrew people, and only the Hebrew people. In fact, there are no objective writings to confirm the claims of the Bible. There is nothing from any source outside of the Hebrew people, to back-up any of their fantastical claims—claims of miraculous victories, of racial superiority, of all the plagues their God dished out to their enemies, of angels or even God Himself visiting the Hebrew leaders, such as Noah, Abraham, Jacob, and Moses. Why wouldn't the Egyptians have written about the divine powers Moses exhibited? More importantly, if God had chosen one race out of all other races of people, why wouldn't He have let the rest of us in on His plan? If a man has three sons, and he wants one of them to be in charge of the others, would he not tell his other two sons to listen to their brother? Would he just tell one son, "Okay, you're in charge now," without letting the other two know what was going on? Sounds like a recipe for disaster to me!

This was one of the main issues I had with the doctrine of the Twelve Tribes Communities. Their entire perspective on race and culture had been difficult to swallow, but then there was the issue of personal preference. Presumably, Yonéq was filled with the Holy

Spirit, so even though it was blatantly obvious that his teachings seemed to be coming from his personal preferences (i.e. he didn't like it when women got too fat, or when Mexicans come to America without conforming to American culture, or when his corn wasn't sweet enough), I was expected to believe that they were what the Holy Spirit wanted me to hear.

It had been easy for me to believe the community when they taught me that Christianity was fallen-away, and not connected to the Holy Spirit, considering the long, bloody history of the Church, but it wasn't as easy to believe them when they'd told me that the Bible was the inerrant, objective word of God. How could personal preference not have tainted the Bible in some way? How could it not have been tampered with? At the same time the community cult tells you that Christianity is fallen-away, they defend the Bible that has been manipulated by the same fallen-away church they are criticizing. Sure, they point out where the translators have erred, but what about the Bible itself? By that I mean, the selection of which books made it into the Bible and which ones were omitted. Am I supposed to trust the Catholic church with their selection of which books are deemed holy and which ones are not? Was the selection of the Bible all a matter of the Pope's personal preference?

The canonization, as this collecting-of-the-books would come to be known, was a gradual process, but it is clear that both the Old

Testament and New Testament books were not canonized until after the First Council of Nicaea, in 325 AD.[48] The community considers this council to be the official, ungodly marriage of church and state, and they do not believe that anybody who lived after these councils had the Holy Spirit until Yonéq. They teach that the emperor should have had nothing to do with these councils, and yet it was Constantine, emperor of Rome, who had gathered the Christian bishops together to settle the controversies that had taken place within the church. They point to John 18:36 as proof that the church should have nothing to do with the government:

Jesus answered, "My kingdom is not of this world. If My kingdom were of this world, My servants would fight, so that I should not be delivered to the Jews; but now My kingdom is not from here."

The Twelve Tribes Communities also greatly criticize Saint Augustine, even going as far as to say that his legacy was the pedophile priest scandal within the Catholic church. This claim is based on the fact that it was Augustine who introduced the Catholic doctrine that "…it is possible that a man should receive faith even from one that is faithless, if he be not aware of the faithlessness of the giver." In other words, even if a priest is in sin, or has become faithless, as long as his followers are unaware of this fact, he can continue to perform his priestly duties. The Twelve Tribes teach that, as a result of this doctrine created by Augustine, bishops and cardinals have often allowed pedophile priests to continue to serve in the church, and have purposefully hidden their crimes from the public. Interestingly enough, it was Augustine who ruled over the councils which determined the New Testament books that would be canonized. [49]I'm not sure how the community fails to see this blatant contradiction, but one thing is clear: They'd tell you that Augustine was not filled with the Holy Spirit, not even when he ruled over these councils. They believe that Augustine was filled with an evil spirit and doing the works of the devil, not of God.

The books that comprise both the New and Old Testament of the Bible, were generally agreed upon by Christian leaders by the 5th century. Every council prior to this time simply affirmed what the Church had already agreed upon.[50] So, while we do not know for sure who all was involved in determining which books would be included in the Bible, we do know that it was decided between 325 and 400 AD. While these dates might not mean much to most Christians, it is particularly troublesome for the Twelve Tribes Community's doctrine, and it is something that I had considered before leaving the community. If you are to base your entire life on one book, you should at least be able to trust its source. It shouldn't have been a matter of preference—which books Augustine and others involved in those councils liked the most. For that matter, how can I trust that the people who wrote those books weren't just writing from their own personal preferences? The truth is I can't, and I don't.

People are entitled to have their own personal preferences. They are even entitled to prefer one culture over another, even over all others! They can even be racist if they want to. They'll be an asshole for it, but they can do it. What people are not entitled to do is to force others to believe what they do. Nobody has the right to take away an innocent person's personal liberty. Yet, throughout history, Jews, Africans, Native Americans, and indigenous people all over the globe have had their personal liberties stripped from them, reduced to slavery, or even killed, on the basis that the creator of the entire universe had somehow chosen one group over all others.

9

THE SIZE OF THE UNIVERSE

Of old You laid the foundation of the earth,

And the heavens are the work of Your hands.

They will perish, but You will endure;

Yes, they will all grow old like a garment;

Like a cloak You will change them,

And they will be changed.

But You are the same,

And Your years will have no end. (Psalm 102: 25-27)

Scientists have not yet pinned down the actual size of the universe, and they may not ever be able to. We still don't know if the universe is infinite or finite, which is what would determine whether it could ever be measured. We have, however, observed a section of the universe that is 13.8 billion light-years away from Earth.[51] Of course, if the universe is a sphere, and we were at its center, then 13.8 billion light-years would just be its radius. However, the universe is also expanding, so by now it is probably much larger. Also, we're most likely not the center of the universe, although many of us would like to think we are. Some scientists believe the universe is a sphere which has a diameter of more than 92 billion light-years.[52] So, while it's unclear what shape it is, or how big it is, we do know that it is incredibly vast, and the fact that we have observed a section of it that is 13.8 billion light-years away is thoroughly impressive!

When we measure things in light-years we are speaking about almost incomprehensible distances. Light travels extremely fast! It travels at 186,000 miles per second.[53] Light from the sun reaches our planet in just over 8 minutes, even though the sun is on average, 93 million miles from Earth.[54] The distance of just one light-year, expressed in miles, is about 5.88 trillion.[55] Multiply that by 13.8 billion, and you've got the farthest section of universe that we have observed. Then multiply that by the rate the universe is expanding by how long it has been expanding, and imagine that distance as the radius of a sphere, or whatever shape you think our universe is. Bottom line: It's huge! And it may not even be the only one; there could be multiverses!

Most of what we have observed in this vast universe has been seemingly random, violent, chaotic, and inhospitable to life. The Twelve Tribes Communities do not believe that there is any life at all out there. They believe that our tiny little planet is the only place where life exists, but that God will change that, like a man changes a cloak, and at the end of the next age, which is the beginning of the eternal age, there will be a new heaven and a new earth.

Now I saw a new heaven and a new earth, for the first heaven and the first earth had passed away. Also there was no more sea.

Then I, John, saw the holy city, New Jerusalem, coming down out of heaven from God, prepared as a bride adorned for her husband.

And I heard a loud voice from heaven saying, "Behold, the tabernacle of God is with men, and He will dwell with them, and they shall be His people. God Himself will be with them and be their God.

And God will wipe away every tear from their eyes; there shall be no more death, nor sorrow, nor crying. There shall be no more pain, for the former things have passed away." (Revelation 21:1-4)

As much as I would love for these verses to be true (no more death, sorrow, or crying), I would love for the community to be proven wrong. I would love to see the little (or big) green (or grey) men (or women, hermaphrodites, or whatever) when they step out of their flying saucer (or teacup) for the first time! It would be incredible to meet another species from a different planet, moon, space station, or wherever. The possibilities are endless! The universe is probably teeming with life, and we just haven't seen it yet, because of the vastness of space. When it does happen, and I do believe it will be soon, the community will have to admit they are wrong, and then they can join the rest of us out here in the world and get on with life. That would be nice, and I'd be happy for my old friends to finally be free of their confinement, but what I would be even more thrilled about would be the first contact with an alien species! My hope is that they'd be peaceful, and much smarter than us and would be able to set the record straight, once-and-for-all, on all these differences we've been fighting over for all these millennia. It would make all the petty little things we argue about, including religion, race, and gender, seem so insignificant.

Given the size of the universe, there are most likely trillions of intelligent aliens out there. We humans tend to think we're the smartest, the best, or even God's chosen ones, but given the odds, that doesn't seem likely. Any god powerful enough to have created the universe as big as it is, is likely unaware of our existence. He may have created all life in the beginning, but we've evolved apart from Him. Also, it's probably not a "Him" but an "it." If there is a creator, or creators, it or they might not be among the thousands of gods humans have invented. Given that we humans have invented thousands of different gods, or even billions if you consider that each individual has their own idea of who God is, the likelihood of guessing the right one out of just the ones we've invented is pretty slim. But that's just among all the gods we've invented here on Earth. What about the possibility that aliens might have invented their own gods as well? What if there really is one true God, among all the trillions or gazillions of gods that have been invented throughout the universe? What if there is someone who is right about who God is? Do you suppose such a god would hold you accountable for not believing in it when your odds of picking just the right god are a gazillion-to-one? Would such a god sentence you to an eternity of torment? He would if He was the god of the Bible.

*"...But the cowardly, **unbelieving**, abominable, murderers, sexually immoral, sorcerers, idolaters, and all liars shall have their part in the lake which burns with fire and brimstone, which is the second death."* (Revelation 21: 8)

"You shall have no other gods before Me.

You shall not make for yourself a carved image—any likeness of anything that is in heaven above, or that is in the earth beneath, or that is in the water under the earth; you shall not bow down to them nor serve them. For I, the Lord your God, am a jealous God, visiting the iniquity of the fathers upon the children to the third and fourth generations of those who hate Me,

but showing mercy to thousands, to those who love Me and keep My commandments." (Exodus 20: 3-6)

It would be virtually impossible to win this intergalactic God lottery, so the vast majority of us would be doomed to an eternity of torment, just like all the people here on Earth—Native Americans, Africans, and non-European indigenous people—who lived and died before the missionaries were kind enough to show up, take their land, rape their women, and bring them the "good news" of their savior. Just like those who've lived and died here on Earth who never had the opportunity to hear about the "one true God," we earthlings who never heard of the God of a civilization 36 million light-years away from us would be doomed to eternity of agony in a burning lake of fire if their god were like the god of the Bible. Fortunately, such a scenario does not exist outside of our pathetically primitive human minds. If it did exist, I would not be participating in the God lottery, for such a God would not be worthy of anybody's love, faith, belief, or whatever else it is that humans think they are giving to their gods, as if the creator of the entire universe is in need of anything a mere human could give them. Am I expected to believe God created the universe, more than 92 billion light-years across, and His primary concern—the first commandment, is to not have any other gods before Him—that He's a jealous god, and that if I don't believe in Him I'll be sent to a lake of fire? Am I really expected to believe that? Because I don't. It's a really stupid concept, and very clearly man-made. It's a concept that was invented by ignorant, power-hungry, primitive men who are not worthy of being followed or honored in any way. Sadly though, I believed this for nearly eight years. I wasted a large chunk of my life serving people who fed me these ridiculous lies. I can only hope that other people will read this and not get duped in the same way I was.

Now that I've made it abundantly clear why I no longer believe in the god of the Bible, what about the creator-god? The community believes God created everything for a purpose. When I began to doubt this concept, my first question was, "Why do men have nipples?" Then I wonder why there are self-reproducing hermaphrodite creatures.[56] I wonder what the community would say about that— probably something to the effect of creation being fallen due to "the fall of man." In other words, Eve ate the fruit of a tree and so God told a bunch of hermaphrodite creatures to go fuck themselves.

People who believe in a creator like to point out that if we were any closer to the sun, we'd burn-up and if we were any farther away, we'd freeze. "How do you explain that?" they'll say, as if our planet's perfectly-placed position in our solar system wouldn't have been possible had the creator not made it that way. In reality, the earth regularly shifts, every year in fact, as it orbits the sun, closer and farther away by a range of about 3.1 million miles.[57] This is, in terms of the size of the universe, a very small range, but does that necessarily mean that the creator made it that way? While some would say that the earth was placed here for us, I would argue that we are here because we can be. Where else could we have evolved except in a place that is hospitable for life? Intelligent life-forms on other planets might be considering these very same things, asking themselves, "How did we get here? Did our creator make this planet for us, or are we simply here because it's the only place we could have evolved?"

So then, how did the universe come to be, if it were not created? What went bang? Was it just a bunch of atoms floating around in nothingness until they collided and exploded? In string theory, there is not just one universe, but many universes, floating around like bubbles, and our universe came about as a result of two universe bubbles bouncing into each other, or perhaps a bubble giving birth to a little baby bubble, which is the universe we live in.[58] So, then one might ask, "Who created this bubble bath of universes?" Well, was it the god of the Hebrews? Probably not. The truth is, I cannot disprove the existence of a creator-god, any more than someone can prove its existence. But I can say with certainty that such a creator can be nothing like what people have imagined.

Every version of the creator-god has been imagined by the human brain, and considering this causes me to have even more questions: Where does original thought come from? Are thoughts placed inside our heads by opposing forces? Are all thoughts either good or evil? I believe that we have evolved, equipped with a brain that is powerful enough to imagine—to take what we have learned through external stimulation, and expound upon it. Our experiences, what we feel, what we sense, and what we are taught, all add to our mental capacity. We are capable of sitting down and creating an entire world, a universe, or even multiverses inside of our heads, but this is all due to our ability to evolve. Life cannot be merely a battle of good and evil forces, putting thoughts into our heads, because there are just too many things that are neither good nor evil. They just are. There are so many choices we can make throughout our day and throughout our lives, and while a theist might argue that each choice we make is a matter of good or evil, that we can either choose God or the devil, I would say that most choices are of little to no significance when considering the scale of the universe. Choices like, "What color shirt should I wear?" "What type of tea should I drink?" The universe simply does not care. Wear what you want to. Drink whatever you want to drink. Have some whiskey if you want to—even if it is 10:00 am! Just do it in moderation, because what your experiences have taught you should give you all the wisdom you need to make the right decisions for yourself. Treat others the way that you would want to be treated, not because that's what it says in the Bible, but because experience has taught us that it is the right thing to do—for ourselves, for those around us, and for our entire civilization.

10

RELIGION VERSUS MORALITY

And the Lord God commanded the man, saying, "Of every tree of the garden you may freely eat; but of the tree of the knowledge of good and evil you shall not eat,

for in the day that you eat of it you shall surely die." (Genesis 2:16-17)

According to the Bible, humanity began with Adam and Eve. Eve was tempted with this forbidden fruit, which was the tree of the knowledge of good and evil. A snake lied to her, telling her that she will not die if she eats from it. So, she ate the fruit and God cursed the snake, Eve, and Adam for this egregious affront to His sensibilities. How dare we seek after this knowledge of good and evil! As a result, snakes were doomed to crawl around on their bellies forever, women would suffer increased pain in child birth, and men would have to work hard. Also, God cast both Adam and Eve out of the garden forever, "lest they also eat from the tree of life."

Then the Lord God said, "Behold, the man has become like one of Us, to know good and evil. And now, lest he put out his hand and take also of the tree of life, and eat, and live forever"

— therefore the Lord God sent him out of the garden of Eden to till the ground from which he was taken.

So He drove out the man; and He placed cherubim at the east of the garden of Eden, and a flaming sword which turned every way, to guard the way to the tree of life. (Genesis 3:22-24)

Why did He not want us to know good and evil? Was it insecurity? Was it because we'd be able to judge Him, based on moral principles, and determine that He's a fraud, a killer, a rapist, an enslaver, a torturer, and a racist genocidal maniac? To be sure, the god of the Bible is all of those things, but no, I do not believe He acted in this way out of insecurity. I believe He acted this way because it's just a story, and perhaps the religious leaders who wrote this story did not want people's knowledge to hinder them from accepting the bullshit they were being fed. Perhaps this story was a warning to all of us: If we attempt to know good and evil, right from wrong, we'll be cursed. That might be an effective threat when you have an agenda to push and people are naïve enough to believe you.

Moving on with the story, Adam, Eve, and all of their descendants got busy with populating the earth. Unfortunately, after a short time had passed (in God years), God decided to pay us humans a visit again and he did not like what He saw, which is bad news if you're a human.

Then the Lord saw that the wickedness of man was great in the earth, and that every intent of the thoughts of his heart was only evil continually.

And the Lord was sorry that He had made man on the earth, and He was grieved in His heart.

So the Lord said, "I will destroy man whom I have created from the face of the earth, both man and beast, creeping thing and birds of the air, for I am sorry that I have made them." (Genesis 6:5-7)

At this point, God decided Noah would build a boat, gather his family and two of every kind of animal, and everybody else—every man, woman, child, and yes, even all the babies on the planet, would be killed in a global flood. Noah, his wife, his three sons, and all of their wives were spared, but nobody else. All the nursing babies were drowned by this benevolent, all-powerful, and all-loving god, because apparently, "every intent of the thoughts of their hearts was only evil continually." Those goddamned babies! Always thinking their evil thoughts! Flood them all! It's okay, though, because after the flood, God gave us institutional race-based slavery.

It would only be fair to point out at this time that many Christians believe that we wouldn't even have morality if it weren't for the

Bible. We wouldn't even have modern society if not for the Bible. Just look at the ten commandments! Surely we humans didn't know not to kill before Moses gave us the ten commandments, right? Well, that's partially right: Moses didn't know not to kill before he gave us the ten commandments.

> *Now it came to pass in those days, when Moses was grown, that he went out to his brethren and looked at their burdens. And he saw an Egyptian beating a Hebrew, one of his brethren.*
>
> *So he looked this way and that way, and when he saw no one, he killed the Egyptian and hid him in the sand.*
>
> *And when he went out the second day, behold, two Hebrew men were fighting, and he said to the one who did the wrong, "Why are you striking your companion?"*
>
> *Then he said, "Who made you a prince and a judge over us? Do you intend to kill me as you killed the Egyptian?"*
>
> *So Moses feared and said, "Surely this thing is known!" When Pharaoh heard of this matter, he sought to kill Moses.*
>
> *But Moses fled from the face of Pharaoh and dwelt in the land of Midian; and he sat down by a well.* (Exodus 2:11-15)

Moses had to flee, because there was already a law against killing people in ancient Egypt[59], as there was a law against killing people in every successful civilization, mostly because it is just common sense.

I mean, who would build all of Pharaoh's sand castles if everybody was busy killing each other? Of course he wouldn't have wanted his people going around killing each other all the time! So, no, the ten commandments were not the first writings to outlaw murder. The oldest known law code which survives today is the Sumerian code of Ur-Nammu, written between 2100 and 2050 BC, and yes, it does outlaw murder, as well as theft.[60]

But what about the other commandments? Surely they were beneficial to modern society, right? No, actually. They weren't. Not in the least bit. Not only do we have no need of them, because we have common sense by which we can write our modern laws, the first four commandments had nothing to do with society:

"I am the Lord your God, who brought you out of the land of Egypt, out of the house of bondage.

"You shall have no other gods before Me.

"You shall not make for yourself a carved image—any likeness of anything that is in heaven above, or that is in the earth beneath, or that is in the water under the earth;

you shall not bow down to them nor serve them. For I, the Lord your God, am a jealous God, visiting the iniquity of the fathers upon the children to the third and fourth generations of those who hate Me,

but showing mercy to thousands, to those who love Me and keep

My commandments.

"You shall not take the name of the Lord your God in vain, for the Lord will not hold him guiltless who takes His name in vain.

"Remember the Sabbath day, to keep it holy. Six days you shall labor and do all your work, but the seventh day is the Sabbath of the Lord your God.

In it you shall do no work: you, nor your son, nor your daughter, nor your male servant, nor your female servant, nor your cattle, nor your stranger who is within your gates.

For in six days the Lord made the heavens and the earth, the sea, and all that is in them, and rested the seventh day. Therefore the Lord blessed the Sabbath day and hallowed it. (Exodus 20:2-11)

Imposing such laws on modern society would be morally repugnant. We already know what happened to good-intentioned people in the past who found themselves inadvertently disobeying these laws, and we do not want to bring such injustices back to our present time.

Now while the children of Israel were in the wilderness, they found a man gathering sticks on the Sabbath day.

And those who found him gathering sticks brought him to Moses and Aaron, and to all the congregation. They put him under guard, because it had not been explained what should be done to him.

229

Then the Lord said to Moses, "The man must surely be put to death;
all the congregation shall stone him with stones outside the camp."

So, as the Lord commanded Moses, all the congregation brought
him outside the camp and stoned him with stones, and he died.
(Numbers 15:32)

Throughout history, as religion became too powerful, to the point of gaining control of the government, injustices such as this have taken place—people being burned at the stake for claiming that the earth revolves around the sun,[61] drowned for gathering herbs,[62] being accused of witchcraft[63], stabbed, beaten, strangled to death[64] for being Jewish, and the list goes on and on. The founders of the United States of America were escaping such a state religion, which restricted their freedoms, and that is why we have religious freedom in this country. The separation of church and state was not established, as many modern Christians presume, to protect the church from the state, but to protect the people from the murderous church.[65]

So, four commandments had nothing to do with modern society and laws against murder and theft already existed, so then that just leaves honoring your parents, not committing adultery, not lying, and not coveting. Would humanity know not to do these things were it not for the commandments? Should modern societies have laws to enforce these things? On the issue of honoring your parents, that's instinctual, especially if you were raised by parents that are worthy of honor and who enforce their authority. Adultery is not a state issue, but I would say that if you don't want to be an asshole you shouldn't cheat on your partner. It's kind of a basic human principle and it certainly wasn't invented by the Bible. Of course, it's not cheating if you have an open relationship and your partner knows what is going on, or perhaps they are participating in your sexual adventures with other people. This is also something that the government should have no involvement with. Not lying? That too is a basic human principle, but in some cases, lying is necessary, like when the religious police come along and ask you if your friend was gathering sticks on the Sabbath. "Nope, no sticks here." Last on the list is coveting. Coveting? What are we, the thought police? Of course there shouldn't be a law against coveting! To say we wouldn't have the modern society we have without the ten commandments would be outrageous.

What about the rest of the Bible? Doesn't the Bible teach us all the things we know about morality? There are two stories in the Bible that begin with a gang of bisexual men who want to rape another man, but they are offered women to rape instead, because it's wrong to rape men, but it's fine if it's a woman. The story in Genesis 19 is the one that is most often quoted. In that story, two angels, who looked like men, go down to Sodom, where Lot shows them hospitality and brings them into his house. Then the men of Sodom surround Lot's house and demand that he bring out the men who are really angels so they can have sex with them, but Lot offers them his virgin daughters instead. In that story, the girls were spared from being raped, because the angels blinded the men of Sodom and they couldn't find the door. Even though that story ends with both Sodom and Gomorrah being completely destroyed and Lot's wife is turned into a pillar of salt for looking back, I find the story in Judges 19 to be even more disturbing.

In Judges 19, a man from the tribe of Levi was travelling through the tribe of Benjamin with his concubine. As night fell, they were fortunate enough to have met an old man who showed them hospitality and allowed them to stay in his house. However, the men of that city surrounded the house and demanded that the old man bring out the Levite man who was staying with him so they could have sex with him. But the old man offers the bisexual gang his virgin daughter and the Levite's concubine to "humble them." He then says that doing this to a man would be "a vile thing!" When they do not answer the old man, the Levite brings out his concubine instead. They rape her all night and she passes-out, so the Levite cut her into twelve pieces and distributed each piece to each of the Twelve Tribes. This starts a civil war and the story ends in Judges 21, with the Israelites arranging for the men of Benjamin to marry their virgin daughters. They do this by instructing the men of Benjamin to hide in the vineyards and watch for dancing girls and every man was to grab a girl for himself and make her his wife. This was done, because the civil war had left the tribe of Benjamin devastated and they needed to reproduce or there would no longer be twelve tribes, thus, their religion/nation would die, because they need all twelve tribes to be God's people.

What can we learn about morality from these stories? That it's okay to rape a woman, but not a man? Is it okay to rape young girls if you are doing so to save your religion? Christians will say that the story in Judges happened because "there was no king in the land." (Judges 19:1) I see. This is prophetic! Now Jesus is our king, so we don't need to rape people anymore! So, I'm expected to believe that without Jesus, people are just going around raping, killing, eating their own babies (2 Kings 6:28-29), and all the other morally repugnant things described in the Bible? What about all the other civilizations on the planet? Were they just as morally corrupt as ancient Israel? All of them? The Chinese, Africans, Native Americans, Aborigines—all baby eating, little girl raping, murderous, soulless bastards? I don't think so. When it comes to morality, the Bible describes one of the most corrupt civilizations in the history of our planet. And we're expected to accept the Bible as our source for morality? People were doing just fine in other parts of the world. They didn't need the Bible to tell them how to be good people. Especially when it was brought to them by violent men wearing full metal armor and wielding swords.

But what about the golden rule? Treat other people the way you would want to be treated. We certainly wouldn't have that without Jesus, right? The concept of Karma began to be taught prior to 1500 BC.[66] The oldest written Hindu text appears at this time and speaks of Karma—the concept that if you do good deeds, good things will come to you, but if you do bad deeds, bad things will come to you. In other words, it is saying, "You should treat people the way you would want to be treated, and here's why…" Once again, it is a basic human principle. Not only was it taught all throughout Asia, but there are also many Native American[67] [68]and African[69] teachings which enforce the same concept. People everywhere knew this to be true. All the successful civilizations throughout history survived as long as they did, because of the fact that the majority of their populations lived by this principle. So, no, you do not need Jesus, or God, or the Bible to be a good person. You can just be good because you want to be—not because you are being threatened with eternal damnation, or expecting an eternal reward for your good behavior. Yes, there are consequences for bad behavior in this life, and rewards for good behavior. This motivates most people in modern societies to at least not do the horrible things that people did throughout the Old Testament, but beyond that, many people actually choose to be good on their own. Some people will choose to do good deeds, even when they are not expecting a reward, and they choose to not to do the bad things they could do, even when nobody is watching. This is called integrity. Some people have it, and some don't. Whether someone possesses integrity or not has nothing to do with one's religious affiliation.

In the interest of being fair and balanced, I will point out that there are many teachings from the Bible that I do believe are morally sound, such as the Bible's focus on caring for the poor and needy.

A father to the fatherless, a defender of widows,
is God in his holy dwelling.
God makes a home for the lonely;

He leads out the prisoners into prosperity,
Only the rebellious dwell in a parched land. (Psalm 68:5-6)

What I like most about how the Bible addresses the issue of poverty and income inequality, is that it doesn't just leave it up to God, as it could have, but rather, it exhorts those who have wealth to care for those who do not.

But whoever has the world's goods, and sees his brother in need and closes his heart against him, how does the love of God abide in him? (1 John 3:17)

Jesus said to him, "If you want to be perfect, go, sell what you have and give to the poor, and you will have treasure in heaven; and come, follow Me." (Matthew 19:21 and a slightly different version in Mark 10:21)

Now, if you were to ask a modern Christian why they did not give up all their possessions to follow Jesus, they would probably tell you that it was just for the rich young ruler (the story in Matthew 19 and Mark 10), or they'll tell you that it was for back then. I'd agree that it was for back then, as was the rest of the Bible. It was written for another people in another time. It should not be used as our moral guide book for modern times. However, does that mean that we shouldn't care for the needy, that we should let children starve to death while we amass wealth for ourselves? One of the most outrageous and sad realities of our time is that our heroes are billionaires. We somehow think that because they're wealthy, that means they're smart, or that they are worthy of our admiration. I don't know what world these people who idolize billionaires are living in. Maybe in their fairy world, where unicorns fart rainbows and puke candy, billionaires got to where they are through hard work and sacrifice, but here on Earth, all the billionaires got that way by being heartless and letting children starve. It is unethical to be a billionaire in a world where children are starving to death.

As I write this, there are children on this planet who are sitting in their own filth, naked, and suffering immensely with hunger pains or dehydration. Their arms are thin, frail, and weak, and their guts are distended. How can we allow this to happen? How are people okay with this? These children didn't choose to be born into such a cruel, unloving, and unforgiving world—to be born into a short lifetime of suffering, knowing nothing but pain. They are so small and fragile. They are vulnerable, entirely dependent, and innocent. Without anyone to help them, they are left thinking that no one loves them and that nobody cares, and are they wrong? When I first held my son, he was so small and fragile. He was vulnerable, entirely dependent, and innocent. I didn't want anything bad to ever happen to him. I know that there are bound to be hardships in life, and that these hardships build character, but I did not want my son to ever suffer needlessly. I wanted him to always be safe, warm, well-fed, and well cared for. I wanted him to be secure and to always know that he is loved, just as every child should. How can somebody be a billionaire when there are children that don't even have their basic needs met? How do these people not care? I want so badly to be able to do something to end global poverty, but there is very little I could do in my current position. These billionaires that we idolize, they could do something, more than any of the rest of us, but they choose instead to selfishly hoard their wealth, or to give a tiny percentage of it and boast about the millions that they've given away. One billion dollars is a thousand million! It's a shit-ton of money—way more than anybody could possibly need! These billionaires are so deceived thinking that they are good people when they have the power to alleviate needless suffering for millions of people and they don't. Just do something already! Stop trying to justify your worthless, immoral extravagance and fucking do something!

Some have tried to be charitable and have failed miserably. It's really not that hard though, if you logically address the problems, to come up with solutions that work. For example, if you were to try to tackle the issue of wide-spread poverty and illness during the peak of the AIDS epidemic, you might think a logical first step would be to hand out condoms and teach people to use them. At least that could be done in conjunction with providing food and medical services. It's quite simple: First, by providing condoms, you'd be helping to prevent the spread of sexually infectious diseases, and secondly, you'd be preventing more babies from being born into poverty. This would result in fewer mouths to feed, which would mean more food to go around, which means those babies who are already born would get to eat.

This seems like such a simple solution you'd think all the charities would've done it, right? Well, unfortunately, the Catholic church, which is often praised for their charitable works, did exactly the opposite. In the midst of the AIDS epidemic, they taught people not to use protection, because contraception is banned according to their doctrine.[70] [71] This exacerbated the AIDS crises, resulted in even more mouths to feed, which they couldn't keep up with, and a much greater amount of human suffering (which they think is a good thing).[72] You'd think they'd at least prioritize pain relief when providing medical treatment to help alleviate some of the suffering, but nope. They teach that the suffering is good for the soul and helps you get to heaven. Too bad that's not a real place and the Bible doesn't actually say you'll go to heaven when you die, otherwise they might be on to something!

What would Jesus do? This is the question people love to ask, but hate to answer. He'd accumulate unlimited wealth in a world with finite resources, wouldn't He? If you're a wealthy Christian in America, then yes, that is exactly what Jesus would do, because Jesus hates the goddamn Commies! If you take Him at His word, however, He'd do the exact opposite—making Himself poor for the sake of others.

And Jesus said to him, "Foxes have holes and birds of the air have nests, but the Son of Man has nowhere to lay His head." (Matthew 8:20 and Luke 9:58)

The bible very clearly describes a community, in which the early believers gave up all that they had—all their possessions, in their devotion to God. Not only can this be found in Acts 2:44-45 and 4:32-35, but it was apparently so important to the early Christians, that they included a story of a man and his wife who held back some of their possessions, lied about it, and were killed by God as a result. This story can be found in Acts 5:1-11. It paints a clear picture of the choice early disciples had to make: They could keep their possessions for themselves and live a comfortable life (Acts 5:4), or they could give all their possessions to the community in order to follow Jesus. They couldn't do both. There are those today who make a very decent living lying to people and trying to distort this written history. They twist so much of the Bible, severely disfiguring it, until it finally fits into their gospel of prosperity. If they can change so much of what the Bible says, I wonder why they still bother to use it at all.

For the sake of argument, let's humor these fake, lying preachers. Let's say it was for back then, as these hypocrites would have us think. What changed between now and then? Did God change His mind? Or possibly, did the early believers get it wrong, and modern Christians are the ones who are right? It would stand to reason that the most authentic form of any movement can be found at its early days—closer to the movement's founders. Movements tend to degrade over time, growing further apart from the founder's original intentions. In this case, we are talking about a movement founded by the disciples of Jesus—those who were with Him, being taught by Him. They were, according to the Bible, the men who knew Jesus personally. The movement they founded required its followers to give up all their possessions and live in a community. Modern Christianity is horrendously disfigured, completely unrecognizable from the movement established by the first disciples of Jesus.

I'm not advocating the practice of giving up all of one's possessions, as the Twelve Tribes Communities teach. While I do believe that is what a true Christian would do, as this is what the first Christians did, it shouldn't be required of people any more than Christianity should be required. I believe that it's possible to live comfortably

240

and be generous. Here in America, in this present time, the ideal annual income for happiness is about $75,000. That's a comfortable income. Any American can live comfortably on that amount, so why should we have millionaires and billionaires? Provided we were giving to efficient charities, I believe that we could effectively end global poverty if every American making more than $75,000 per year would donate their excess. I've never made that much in a year, not even close, but it's a goal I hope to achieve, and when I do reach that point I will be giving my excess. As it is, I make about $40,000 and I've already donated to several international charities that I feel are efficient and good at what they do. I've got a wife and son to take care of, but if even I can donate, with my meager income, what excuse do millionaires and billionaires have? Especially if they call themselves Christians! Are they going to allow themselves to be outdone by an atheist?

While Christians judge us atheists as being immoral unbelievers, they preach a gospel of prosperity, teaching that when people are wealthy it's because they're blessed, and those who are poor are cursed. They ignore the parts of the Bible that teach the exact opposite, or try to excuse those verses away. They set up their ineffectual charities, not based on practical, real-world solutions, but on religious ideologies which often fail to achieve any real progress and often end up making things worse. This isn't indicative of all Christians. There are, after all, more than 45,000 different denominations of Christianity[73], and not everyone who calls themselves a Christian belongs to one of those denominations. There are a lot of Christians that have a good head on their shoulders. These are the ones that don't judge people based on their religion, but by the content of their character, as one ought to be judged by. So, for these common-sense Christians, and for all the atheists, humanists, and generally descent human beings out there, we can work towards the real-world solutions that will end poverty. If someone is hungry, let's feed them. If they're thirsty, let's give them something to drink. Let's clothe the naked, take care of the sick, and visit the prisoners. I think someone said something about that once. If there's a bunch of idiots roaming the planet, let's educate them! Let's focus on charities that do these things, rather than the ones that push our own religious ideologies, and we'll see where that takes us. We've already seen what religion can accomplish, so let's try something different now.

The problem is, there are some powerful forces holding the world back from progress. Here in America, the policies of the so-called "Christian Right" are a curious blend of ignorance and hypocrisy. It's an extremely powerful movement—a political force that is virtually unrivaled. While early Christian believers were working towards a kingdom that was "not of this world," members of the Christian Right seem to be fighting, in the arena of worldly politics, for a kingdom that is very much of this world.

Jesus answered, "My kingdom is not of this world. If My kingdom were of this world, My servants would fight, so that I should not be delivered to the Jews; but now My kingdom is not from here."
(John 18:36)

Unlike their earlier counterparts who were non-violent, peace-loving, communal-living, devoted believers, these modern Christians are politically active; they fight in wars; they accumulate massive amounts of wealth, storing up treasures for themselves here on earth. Rather than having their hearts set on their treasures in heaven, they seem to be hellbent on creating their own nation, based on their own man-made politics. They might judge people like me who don't believe in the god of the Bible, but they don't believe in the god of the Bible either. They believe in the god that their lying leaders made up for them.

Some of the Christian Right's policies include deporting illegal immigrants (which naturally targets brown-skinned people from "shit-hole" countries, rather than light-skinned people from countries like Norway), supporting the unlimited accumulation of wealth at all costs, opposing income tax increases on the wealthy, giving globs of money to Israel, supporting Israel's military with money collected from American's income taxes, and opposing environmental regulations, allowing corporations to destroy our planet. For anyone who considers themselves to be part of this Christian Right movement, I've got some questions: Do you not know that according to Revelation 11:18, your god will destroy those who destroy the earth? When your loving God looks down at poor children from Syria, or Mexico, or Africa, or Haiti, or any of the other "shit-hole" places you despise, do you think He sees filthy foreigners that deserve to rot in hell? Do you not know that the Twelve Tribes were scattered abroad?[74] Do you not know that they could have gone to Assyria, which included the area that is now modern-day Syria? The Syrian refugees you despise could be the descendants of the ones your god called "a chosen people."[75] They could be just as much "sons of the covenant"[76] as the Israelis you love so much! Do you not know that the descendants of the missing tribes could have spread throughout the whole world by now? The foreigners you despise so much could be the descendants of Abraham, Isaac, and Jacob, whom your god said would be multiplied "like the stars of the heavens." Here they are! They've multiplied, but how are you treating them? And finally, on the issue of unchecked accumulation of wealth, isn't it possible that eventually, if someone gets good enough at the art of accumulating wealth, that they could accumulate all the world's resources, leaving the rest of us to starve, while you vehemently defend their right to do so? Is it possible that someone could "gain the whole world and lose their soul?"[77] No, that couldn't be possible! The person who said that was an idiot, right? The person who said, "the love of money is the root of all evil"[78] was an idiot, right?

So, yes, I am an atheist. I'm sorry if you are offended that I do not believe in your god, but to be honest, you who call yourselves "Christians" have given me no reason to do so. Your sporadic and misplaced generosity is no consolation for your zealous destruction of the earth, your hatred towards people who are different from you, and your selfish extravagance. You who call yourselves "Christians" can judge me all you want for not believing in your stupid, selfish, made-up god, but then you'd be solidifying your hypocrisy even more. Or was it also an idiot who said not to judge, lest you be judged?[79]

What if I'm wrong? If I'm wrong, and the god of the Bible is real, then I'll be tortured in a fiery lake for eternity. I don't think one can morally justify such a punishment for any crime, much less the crime of being wrong, but that's what the Bible says. The unbelievers are doomed to suffer in this way for eternity.[80] I do not believe in such a god, not just because His existence is highly improbable, but because I want nothing to do with a cruel, abusive monster who is so egotistical that He would force His creation to worship Him and no one else, at the threat of eternal punishment. You would think that an almighty god would have been able to arrange for some sort of reformative therapy for "the bad guys" instead of eternal torment without hope of restoration, but not according to the Bible. The Bible seems to imply that once you die, you'll be judged based on how you've lived your life, and there is no longer any hope for reformation—ever.[81] It's certainly an effective fear tactic, but not enough to make a believer out of me!

II

I AM A BELIEVER!

Being an atheist doesn't mean not believing in anything. Humans are complex. We all have our own unique belief system in place, determining our thoughts, which form our words, influence our actions, and ultimately shape our society. In considering my own beliefs, I imagine a perfect, utopian scenario, something I could put my "faith" in; it involves a cure for all diseases, and even death itself. It involves humanity escaping the smothering confines of our tiny, overpopulated planet and exploring the universe. Some believe that this is something God will do for us, but I see it as something we will have to do for ourselves. It will require significant improvement in education, a great amount of cooperation, and the sharing of our resources.

I believe that we should all be seekers of truth. As we grow in knowledge, and the old doctrines we once believed in no longer stand up against our critical thinking, we should abandon such outdated theologies and press forward to a better future for humanity. We may all have developed our own preconceived ideas and beliefs, but as we are faced with evidence and objective reasoning which contradicts our previously held beliefs, we ought to be willing to change. The ability to adapt is what has aided us humans in survival thus far, so all we need to do is keep up the good work!

The development of the world's various religions was largely influenced by race and culture. These differences once divided us, but we have since learned that we are much more similar than previously thought. While many people once believed that people of other races were sub-human, not even from the same species, but from an inferior species, we now know that genetically, each person is, on average, 99.9% similar to every other human.[82] Also, even though skin color is often emphasized, it is not the most important determining factor of one's race.[83] Consider the fact that the layer of skin which determines one's skin color is only one of five layers in the epidermis,[84] and that the thickness of the entire epidermis ranges from half a millimeter to 1.5 millimeters.[85] Given the fact that we did not choose which race we were born into, race should be of very little significance in our modern culture. Instead, we should all realize, as members of the same human race, that we can all identify, in many ways, to every other human. It is my hope that identifying with one another will lead to a greater, more enlightened, global culture.

I understand that this idea of a global culture is scary to many fundamentalist Christians, causing some to even go so far as to actively work against globalization and unity, but these folks really need to get over themselves. As I've said before, don't let your outdated theologies get in the way of objective reasoning. Many Christians are terrified of the coming Antichrist and his one-world government. As a result, they will be opposed to any concerted efforts towards the global cooperation that will be necessary to achieve such worthy endeavors as an end to war, poverty, and disease. If we are to achieve peace, we need to leave behind the things that divide us. I'm not advocating that we all unite behind one man, as that has been proven, many times before, to be disastrous. I would prefer that each person be given a voice and that each of our voices, collectively, would be the basis for action in our society. If we are able to make significant advancements in education, each person's voice will be that much more effective at improving society. My utopian society is comprised of free-thinking individuals, all equals, and all intellectuals—experts in their chosen fields. This needn't be a scary thought to anyone, but should instead be a source of hope to everyone.

I believe that there most likely were advanced civilizations in the past that we now know nothing about. These societies might have been non-violent and may have focused their intellect on scientific advancements rather than on war. It saddens me to consider all the knowledge that may have been lost when more violent and less intelligent invaders came along. We do know that throughout ancient times and the medieval ages, invading armies leveled cities, smashed artifacts, and burned countless books (The destruction of Jerusalem[86], Constantinople[87], and the library at Alexandria[88] are just a few examples). This has even happened recently in the Middle East.[89]

I cannot imagine how much accumulated knowledge—the result of centuries or even millennia of collaboration between the brightest minds, has been completely lost as a result of all these wars. Many of these wars were a direct result of differences in religious beliefs, and it is the intolerance towards different cultures and beliefs, as well as the desire to preserve religious doctrines, that has provoked people to burn books and destroy knowledge, resulting in most of our history being lost. These were our ancestors that did these things—yours and mine. We, however, have evolved and are evolving. It is my hope that we will move away from having to think about war. Perhaps when we perfect our defenses to the point that we no longer have to think about defense, we will be able to focus instead on space exploration and we will come to understand our universe. Perhaps when we secure our supplies of food and clean water to the point that we no longer have to think about these things, we will focus our intellect on curing all disease.

Even here in America, "the greatest country on Earth," our present society is far from ideal. We have an epidemic of mental illness, and we are doing far too little to address it.[90] The exact causes of mental illness, unfortunately are still unknown.[91] Seeing people who are close to me on a very personal level suffer from mental illness has caused me to believe in the chemical imbalance theory of mental illness. The chemical imbalance theory is still unproven, because the theory does not explain how the chemicals become imbalanced in the first place.[92] But I have seen first-hand, how an episode of mental illness, which society has often viewed as just "bad behavior" can suddenly, without warning, attack a person's brain. I have also seen how medications can treat those attacks. From what I have seen, mental illness attacks people and causes them to behave in ways that they do not wish to behave. That is why it is classified as mental illness and not just bad behavior that needs to be modified through the person's own will-power. People who are truly suffering from mental illness aren't going to be able to modify their own behavior, no matter how much will-power they exert. They need doctors, therapy, medications, and clearly, a lot more research needs to be conducted, so we can fully comprehend all of the various mental illnesses people suffer from and treat them effectively.

In the Twelve Tribes, when an individual suffers from mental illness, most of the time they are treated as though they have an evil spirit. In fact, with most medical conditions in the community, the people suffering from the conditions are seen as "lacking faith." Children growing up in the community who suffer from mental illness are probably spanked more often, and they certainly go undiagnosed, as doctor's visits are limited, and the Twelve Tribes would never accept a diagnosis such as ADHD. They do not believe ADHD is a real disease and they think it can just be spanked out of the child. This is precisely the type of abuse the Twelve Tribes ought to be condemned for.

I often wonder if people who suffer from mental illnesses are like canaries—warning us of critical flaws within society which need to be fixed. While I recognize that there are many legitimate medical conditions which fall under the category of mental illness, I wonder how much of what we call, "mental illness" is, in reality, a normal reaction to an abnormal society. For example, imagine someone is on a stage and about to give a speech or sing a song, but when they open their mouth, they start to choke. People in the audience begin to laugh, and some even mock, so the person on stage begins behaving abnormally. Perhaps they start to scream, or stomp their feet, beat their chest, or otherwise lash-out. While some might consider this type of abnormal behavior to be symptomatic of a mental illness, I believe it is an entirely reasonable response to something within our greater society that is fundamentally flawed.

There are many social constraints, which place an unhealthy amount of pressure on people, causing unbearable stress which inflicts lasting damage. One of the analogies the community loved to use was that of lobsters in a tank, awaiting their inevitable demise. When one lobster attempts to climb up the wall to freedom, the other lobsters latch on to it and drag it down. The community used this analogy to illustrate how sinful people influence others to commit sins. However, my desire for freedom caused me to interpret that analogy differently; I thought about how every time somebody wanted to leave the community, the other members would encircle that person and try to convince them to stay. Then later, those who wanted to leave would be the very same people who'd tried to convince others to stay. I see this behavior in the greater society as well. We all hate to wake up early in the morning and work hard, for long hours, and get little pay to show for it. We see this type of life as a hopeless dead end, and if we were given millions of dollars, we'd quit our jobs in a heartbeat and never work again. Not believing it ourselves, we'll tell others that they should work hard, even if it's at a job they hate, because this is the way they'll achieve success. Rather than working together to build a better society, we'll convince each other to conform to the already existing society, finding it difficult to do so ourselves. In this way, we are strengthening and perpetuating the society we loathe, ensuring the suffering of generations to come—all for the shallow goal of becoming wealthy.

I've never been wealthy, and I have never done much socializing with wealthy people, so I can't speak from experience, but it seems like there are probably many social constraints which wealthy people inadvertently place on other wealthy people. I've never been to a high-end restaurant that offers valet parking, but I imagine someone showing up to one of these fancy valet places in a fifteen-year-old econo-series sedan with rust, chipped paint, and dents all over it, getting out of their car wearing jeans and a stained t-shirt. I don't imagine it would go well for such a person. Or I imagine what would happen if someone weeps, or yells, raises their voice, argues, curses, or in some way exhibits sub-standard behavior for such a "sophisticated" establishment. What if someone shows emotions of some sort, you know, like a normal person? Such a person could not expect to do much socializing among the wealthy. As a result, many feel the need to spend exorbitant amounts of money on status symbols, such as expensive vehicles and clothing, even if it is not what they want. They will smile, even if they feel like weeping. They will keep their voice down, even if they feel like yelling. They'll agree, even when they feel like arguing. This way, they will fit in, and for some, fitting in is more important than anything—even happiness, emotional stability, and physical well-being.

We yearn to be free, expressing our creativity. Our intellect is longing to be challenged and stimulated. Our minds eagerly seek the truth, but the most important thing we seek is love and approval. I wonder how much of what we call, "mental illness," would cease to exist in a society that is tailored to the needs of our minds. Imagine if someone were given the stage, even if for just a moment. Say they were given three minutes, and in those three minutes they were free to express themselves in front of a respectful audience. They could choose to speak, or not to speak. They could choose to sing, or not to sing. If they wanted to, they could scream, stomp their feet, or beat their chest. At the end of their allotted time, the audience would clap, cheer, and affirm the individual who was brave enough to bare their hearts before others, making themselves vulnerable. This is what true freedom would look like. Imagine if you could drive whatever vehicle you wanted to drive, or choose not to have a vehicle. Maybe you'd prefer to walk or ride the bus instead. Imagine if you could wear whatever clothes you wanted to, or choose not to wear clothes if you don't want to. Imagine if you could wear your hair however you wanted to, or choose to be bald. Imagine if you could choose all these things without anybody judging you for your choice. This is what true freedom would look like.

In these examples, I wonder, where's the harm? If someone walks onto a stage and doesn't speak, are they hurting anyone? If someone chooses to drive a cheap sedan instead of the latest luxury model, are they hurting anyone? Why should society punish someone that has done no wrong? Acting weird, being frugal, expressing one's emotions—these are not the types of things that warrant punishment. No, it's the rapists, murderers, child abusers, corrupt government officials, and con artists that deserve to be punished. As cliché as it may sound, we ought to be encouraging people who are simply "being themselves" and not causing any harm to anyone. There is an objective moral standard, one that humanity has known about long before the Bible: we should treat others the way that we would want to be treated.

There are many societal issues that I would love to change. One such example is healthcare in America. There are far too many Americans who believe that owning a gun is a basic human right, but access to affordable healthcare isn't. It is only a barbaric society that would allow its citizens to suffer financially as a result of having been born with a debilitating disease. Yet, that is exactly what I have experienced. I spend too much of my hard-earned money on health care costs, and I have often missed work because of my health. I believe in equal rights for all. Yet, right here in America, "the land of the free," people have had to fight to secure rights that they should have been entitled to. I'll use a recent example: Why did gay couples have to fight so hard for the right to marry? What else besides religious ideology would have caused gay couples to have been denied their rights in the first place? This would have never happened in a secular society based on objective moral principles. Such a society would never tolerate racism, sexism, or inequality. I do not know how to go about changing the world, but I do know that the way society is now is not the way it should be. In many ways, this awareness has been the root of many of my struggles from a very early age. It is because I was so disturbed by the disfunction within the greater society that I joined a cult.

When I first joined the community, the thought I'd had was, "What if everyone in the world lived like this?" After nearly eight years of living in the community, I now have my answer: If the Twelve Tribes ruled the world, there would no longer be any violence. There'd be no poverty. Music and dancing would be greatly esteemed, as would skilled trades and craftsmanship. There'd be no need to fight over religions anymore, as it would be the world's only religion, and the community focuses much of their efforts on coming to one mind in all aspects of life. That said, there'd be some issues. Men and women would not be equal. The races would not be equal. Old and young would not be equal. There would be a strict hierarchy, with the leadership being composed of older males, primarily white, and they would have the power to make every important decision in each of our lives. There would be no freedom to disagree, no freedom of religion, nor freedom of speech. People who are attracted to each other, even people who would be considered legal aged adults in America, would not necessarily be allowed to be together. Homosexuality would be outlawed, as would modern science. There would be no space exploration and little to no advancements in medical science. Though we'd have our basic needs met (for the most part), it would be a dystopian society, as all church-controlled states have been in the past. This is no longer the world I want to work towards, and I regret having given so much of the strength of my youth to the community.

Fortunately, they're not that big, nor powerful, and I doubt they'll be able to continue to bring in large amounts of members going forward. It was my experience that the number of members leaving the community was roughly equal to the number of people coming in. I believe that they will continue in this way for a long time, and will make little to no progress as they go along.

The bigger threat, then, would be the world's major religions, but in my opinion, even those will make little progress, or even shrink, as people become more educated. It seems as though education is the biggest threat to religion, and the biggest contributor to freedom and equality. I'm not even talking about anti-religious education, either. Anti-religious education is indoctrination, just the same as religious education. When I talk about people leaving religious institutions as they become more educated, I'm simply referring to basic education: science, math, history and social sciences, and even language studies. As people learn more about how the world works, how we got to where we are, and the basic concepts that are the building blocks of critical thinking, they will lose interest in the older religions which came about as a way to explain the unexplainable. Many of those "unexplainable" things now have explanations. It's not just that people lose interest, but rather, they stop believing what these religions have been teaching. Religions will have to continue to change their doctrines, to evolve, as people increase in understanding. Religions will have to increasingly abandon old teachings in favor of science, until the day that they become obsolete. This does not mean that individual beliefs or spirituality would become obsolete. Those things may never go away. I wouldn't want them to.

Even after leaving the community, I have maintained a type of spirituality and even mysticism in my life. It stems from a sense of wonder and a "what if" perspective on life and the universe. I love to speculate about the possibilities. I speculate about the universe—about whether there are beings out there who are more powerful than us, smarter, stronger, more compassionate and more loving. I presume that there are. I speculate about life after death. I mean, it's possible. I don't believe it is probable, but it is possible that there is something within our being that will never die, even after our bodies pass away. It's possible, but not probable, that we would pass on into another dimension. This, however, is not what I live for. My goal isn't to make sure my afterlife is better because I was a good person. I live for this present time—to make it better where I am. My goal is to do my best to leave the world better off, even if ever-so-slightly, because I was here.

I consider the power that each of us possesses within ourselves—our "chi" (qi). This is what I believe to be our life-force, and an energy which flows throughout the universe. I do not know to what degree this energy flows, or how much of it makes up our being, but I consider the existence of such energy as both a possibility and a probability. I believe that perhaps our chi is affected by our actions. The choices we make in life can impact the power that flows within and around us. When we do good deeds, we have good chi. When our conscience is clear, our chi is more empowering, but when we know we have done wrong, we often feel powerless. That is why we must go to one another to confess our wrongdoings and do what we can to make things right.

I have developed my own meditative techniques which seem to work well for me. As I mentioned earlier in my story, I'm often able to exercise a relative amount of control over my sickle cell pain by focusing my mental energy on the pain itself. I focus on it, but I try not to react to it. I use deep-breathing techniques and calm my body with my mind. I try to slow everything down and separate my mind from my body, in a way. I use this same technique when I am under a lot of stress, or when I feel myself getting angry. I am by no means perfect at this, but I believe that it has helped me to some extent, and it is something that anybody can do. We all have the power to exercise self-control, controlling our reactions and channeling our negative energy into something positive.

Some may think that not following any particular religion would leave a void in one's life, but that has not been my experience. People are usually concerned about the holidays. What do you celebrate if you're an atheist? Molly and I had this discussion shortly after we had our son. It didn't matter in his first year of life, but we had to consider what we'd teach him as he grew up, and if he'd be missing out on anything. I'd decided that for me, the most important holiday is the New Year. It's the world's most widely celebrated holiday[93], honoring the first day of the Gregorian calendar, which may seem arbitrary, but it is the most commonly used calendar in the world.[94] New Year's Eve, 2017 was the first year we celebrated with Terrence that he was old enough to understand. We watched fireworks celebrations from around the globe. We started watching at around 10:00 am, our time, and it was already 2018 in many parts of the globe, such as Australia and New Zealand. Terrence was four years old at the time, so it was a good opportunity to show him how the world works, with the time zones and the spinning of the globe. When nighttime came in our part of the world, we each had our sparkling beverages, with Molly and I drinking alcohol and Terrence drinking sparkling cider. We ate snacks together, played games, and when our time came, we watched the Times Square ball drop on TV, counted down and then shouted, "Happy New Year!" All these things were things Molly and I had done growing up. We still enjoy it each year, and so will Terrence. He was even more excited about the festivities when we celebrated the 2019 New Year!

We of course, celebrate the Fourth of July, which is our nation's Independence Day. This is the second-most important holiday for me, and a great opportunity to teach Terrence about our nation's history and to be thankful for the freedoms we enjoy. We celebrate this holiday in the traditional ways too—with fireworks and barbeques. I've got nothing against Halloween. Terrence doesn't seem to care why we celebrate it, and neither do I. It's just fun for him to dress up and get candy. As for Thanksgiving, well that's another history-and-thankfulness type of holiday, which we celebrate in the traditional way. Christmas and Easter are the ones I had issues with, but we came up with a solution to the Christmas problem.

Molly and I did not want to lie to our son. We did not tell him that Santa is real, but we did tell him to let his friends believe what they want to. He's not to be a jerk about it and ruin their holiday with the truth. The truth behind Christmas is that it is based on Pagan traditions that existed long before Christianity. Even the date coincides with the winter solstice festivities, which had been celebrated long before Christianity existed.[95] The Roman Christians decided to celebrate the birth of Jesus at this time, even though they didn't know when Jesus was born, and the Bible makes no mention of celebrating birthdays. We decided to celebrate the winter solstice, because it is the true reason for the season. It's simple to explain, too. It's the shortest day of the year, and from that time on, the days begin to get longer. Also, it's a unifying holiday that has been celebrated by many different cultures all around the world.[96] Anyone can celebrate the solstice, regardless of their religious affiliation. Yes, atheists can celebrate Christmas too, but for me, it's hard to get around the "Christ" part. At either rate, both holidays are in close proximity to each other and have many of the same traditions, so we can celebrate along with everyone else.

That said, we do not want to instill greed in our son, making him believe he's entitled to a bunch of presents just because it's a holiday (of course, there's no stopping relatives from burying him in toys). In addition to not wanting to spoil our son, we also don't want to participate in all the Christmas madness. People spend money they don't have on people they barely tolerate, just to honor a fake holiday. They buy a crap-ton of useless trinkets that were made by under-paid, over-worked children overseas.[97] These trinkets have to be shipped, around the globe, burning fossil fuels that are literally making our planet inhospitable.[98] Then these trinkets have to be delivered by stressed-out drivers who have an ungodly amount of pressure placed on them, because everybody wants their packages to arrive all at the same time. When the ungrateful recipients receive their gifts, they are often returned, sometimes requiring even more shipping. It's all complete vanity.

We chose to celebrate the solstice with a feast and treats. Molly makes felt crowns colored orange, yellow, and red to represent the sun, and we light candles. It's a celebration of light, and yes, another opportunity for a history lesson. We don't do anything for Easter. It's such an awkward holiday! There are all these symbols of fertility: colorful eggs, sexually over-active bunnies, chocolate, and Jesus Christ. To each his own, I guess.

I believe that life should be celebrated every day. This is, perhaps, a consequence of not believing that my life was granted to me by a creator-god. It's hard to take your life for granted when you don't believe it was granted. Terrence loves to get squished in a family hug, and we do this pretty much daily as part of our practice of celebrating life. It's not a ritual, it's just a general attitude. We're planning on adopting a child. I don't know if it'll be an older or younger sibling for Terrence, but Molly doesn't want to get pregnant again and there are plenty of children out there that need to be adopted, so that'll be our next step in this celebration of life. We've got plenty of love to share and that's kind of the nature of love. It needs to be shared. You can't keep it to yourself.

So, these are my core beliefs from my inner-most being: always be kind, treating people the way you'd want to be treated, seek the truth, keep learning, and never assume you've already got all the answers. Do all things in moderation—sex is great, as is food, alcohol, spirituality, and generosity, but we should be safe about all these things and never over-do it. With generosity, it is important to make sure your own needs are met first before trying to help others. It is harder to be generous and help others if your own needs are not met. Helping others is much easier when you're in a position to actually do something. That can mean you're in good health or you have a little extra of something (like an extra bedroom for family and friends, or a little extra money to donate to those less fortunate). With spirituality, it should never cause us to ignore the people around us, or somehow justify our misdeeds, but rather, our spirituality should be a way for us to be more connected with reality and accountable for our own deeds. With sex, we must make damn sure it is consensual and safe. Otherwise, we've got no business judging other people's sex lives. Patience is a virtue. Impatient people suck to be around. Violence is never the answer. When it comes to justice, freedom, and peace, don't ever stop fighting. And finally, if someone is in need and you have the power to do something about it, fucking do something!

[1] The International Bible Society, 2011-2019. *Who Wrote the Bible?* [Online] Available at: https://www.biblica.com/resources/bible-faqs/who-wrote-the-bible/

[2] English Club, 1997-2019. History of English. [Online] Available at: https://www.englishclub.com/history-of-english/

[3] The International Bible Society, 2011-2019. *When Was the Bible Written?* [Online] Available at: https://www.biblica.com/resources/bible-faqs/when-was-the-bible-written/

[4] Encyclopedia Britannica, 2019. *Biblical translation.* [Online] Available at: https://www.britannica.com/topic/biblical-translation

[5] (Encyclopedia Britannica, 2019)

[6] Pew Research Center, 2017. *How Americans Feel About Different Religious Groups.* [Online].

[7] Beegle, D. M., 2019. *Moses Hebrew Prophet.* [Online] Available at: https://www.britannica.com/biography/Moses-Hebrew-prophet

[8] Friedman, R. E., 1987. *Who Wrote the Bible.* New York: Summit Books.

[9] Friedman, R. E., 1987. *Who Wrote the Bible.* New York: Summit Books.

[10] Beegle, D. M., 2019. *Moses Hebrew Prophet.* [Online] Available at: https://www.britannica.com/biography/Moses-Hebrew-prophet

[11] The Columbia Encyclopedia, 6th ed., 2019 *Moses* [Online] Available at: https://www.encyclopedia.com/people/philosophy-and-religion/judaism-biographies/moses

[12] (Judges 1:6-7)

[13] Reddie, R., 2007. *Atlantic Slave Trade and Abolition.* [Online] Available at: http://www.bbc.co.uk/religion/religions/christianity/history/slavery_1.shtmldrgaegta

[14] Ojibwa, 2016. *Christian Imperialism.* [Online] Available at: https://nativeamericannetroots.net/diary/2212

[15] The Social Studies Help Center, 2001-2019. *How did the United States justify imperialism?*. [Online] Available at:
http://www.socialstudieshelp.com/usra_imperialism_justify.htm

[16] Fage, J., 1995. A History of Africa. In: *A History of Africa, Third Edition.* London: Routledge, p. 322.

[17] Boahen, A., 1985. General History of Africa - Volume VII - Africa under Colonial Domination 1880-1935. In: General History of Africa - Volume VII - Africa under Colonial Domination 1880-1935. Berkley: UNESCO, p. 12.

[18] Županov, Â. B. Z. a. I. G., 2015. Catholic Orientalism: Portuguese Empire, Indian Knowledge (16th–18th Centuries). In: Catholic Orientalism: Portuguese Empire, Indian Knowledge (16th–18th Centuries). New Delhi: Oxford University Press, pp. 252-259.

[19] Armitage, D., 2012. John Locke: Theorist of Empire?. Department of History, Harvard University.

[20] Runes, D. D., 1965. The Jew and the Cross. In: *The Jew and the Cross.* New York: Citadel Press, p. 61.

[21] Berger, D., 2010. History and Hate: The Dimensions of Anti-Semitism. In: *History and Hate: The Dimensions of Anti-Semitism.* Philadelphia: Jewish Publication Society, p. 69.

[22] Loughlin, J., 1907. The Catholic Encyclopedia. In: *The Catholic Encyclopedia.* New York: Robert Appleton Company, p. "St. Ambrose".

[23] Byrne, D. P., 2017. *Why were the Jews expelled from England in 1290?.* [Online] Available at: https://www.history.ox.ac.uk/::ognode-62416::/files/teaching-resources-expulsion-jews

[24] History of York, 2019. *The 1190 Massacre.* [Online] Available at: http://www.historyofyork.org.uk/themes/norman/the-1190-massacre

[25] Rubin, M., 2004. Gentile Tales: The Narrative Assault on Late Medieval Jews. In: *Gentile Tales: The Narrative Assault on Late Medieval Jews.* Philadelphia: University of Pennsylvania Press, p. 48.

[26] BBC, 2009. *Expulsion of Jews from France in 1306.* [Online] Available at: http://www.bbc.co.uk/religion/religions/judaism/history/expulsionfromfrance.shtml

[27] Sara E. Karesh, M. M. H., 2007. Encyclopedia of Judaism. In: *Encyclopedia of Judaism.* New York: Facts on File, Inc., p. 150.

[28] Foundation for the Advancement of Sephardic Studies and Culture, 1967-2004. *The Edict of Expulsion of the Jews.* [Online] Available at: http://www.sephardicstudies.org/decree.html

[29] Kershner, K., 2017. *In 1492, Spain Forced Jews to Flee the Country or Convert to Christianity.* [Online] Available at: https://history.howstuffworks.com/historical-events/spain-forced-jews-flee-convert-christianity.htm

[30] BBC, 2009. *BBC Religions.* [Online] Available at: http://www.bbc.co.uk/religion/religions/islam/history/spain_1.shtml

[31] Robinson, J. H., 1904. Readings in European History, Volume I. In: *Readings in European History, Volume I.* Boston: Ginn & Company, p. 346.

[32] Douglas Woodruff, I. F. B., 2019. *Saint Pius V.* [Online] Available at: https://www.britannica.com/biography/Saint-Pius-V

[33] Sara E. Karesh, M. M. H., 2007. Encyclopedia of Judaism. In: *Encyclopedia of Judaism.* New York: Facts on File, Inc., p. 150.

[34] Jewish Encyclopedia, 2002-2011. *Popes, The.* [Online] Available at: http://www.jewishencyclopedia.com/articles/3822-bulls-papal-concerning-jews

[35] Kertzer, D. I., 2001. The Popes Against the Jews: The Vatican's Role in the Rise of Modern Anti-Semitism. In: *The Popes Against the Jews: The Vatican's Role in the Rise of Modern Anti-Semitism.* New York: Vintage Books, a division of Random House, p. 27.

[36] The Twelve Tribes believed that the holy spirit revealed the name "Yahshua" to them. They taught that the name "Yah" means "God", and so

it is fitting for the son of God to have "Yah" as part of His name, since it is fitting for the son to have the Father's name.

[37] Scofield Biblical Institute and Theological Seminary, 2019. *YESHUA—How Jesus' name is correctly spelled and what it means.* [Online] Available at: http://scofieldinstitute.org/yeshua-how-jesus-name-is-correctly-spelled-and-what-it-means/

[38] Douglas Harper, 2001-2019. *Online Etymology Dictionary/Jesus.* [Online] Available at: https://www.etymonline.com/word/Jesus

[39] Douglas Harper, 2001-2019. *Online Etymology Dictionary/Christ.* [Online] Available at: https://www.etymonline.com/word/Christ#etymonline_v_11332

[40] Farber, Z., 2016. Images of Joshua in the Bible and Their Reception. In: *Images of Joshua in the Bible and Their Reception.* Berlin: De Gruyter, p. 159.

[41] Lambert, K. R. M. a. R., 2019. *Introduction.* [Online] Available at: http://kingjamesbibletranslators.org/bios/

[42] TIME USA, LLC, 2019. *How the King James Bible Came to Be.* [Online] Available at: http://time.com/4821911/king-james-bible-history/

[43] Shapiro, J., 2016. *How were the Jews regarded in 16th-century England?* [Online] Available at: https://www.bl.uk/shakespeare/articles/how-were-the-jews-regarded-in-16th-century-england

[44] Wood, F., 1990. The Arrogance of Faith. In: *The Arrogance of Faith.* New York: A A Knoopf, p. 59.

[45] Bates, S., 2006. *Church apologises for benefiting from slave trade.* [Online] Available at: https://www.theguardian.com/uk/2006/feb/09/religion.world

[46] LDHI, 2019. *European Christianity and Slavery.* [Online] Available at: http://ldhi.library.cofc.edu/exhibits/show/africanpassageslowcountryadapt/introductionatlanticworld/europnea_christianity_and_slav

[47] National Academy of Sciences, 2019. *Evolution Resources.* [Online] Available at: http://www.nas.edu/evolution/Definitions.html

[48] Hoover, R. W., *How the Canon Was Formed*. [Online] Available at: https://www.westarinstitute.org/resources/the-fourth-r/how-the-canon-was-formed/

[49] McDonald, L. M., 2002. The Canon Debate. In: *The Canon Debate*. Peabody, MA: Hendrickson Publishers, p. 320.

[50] P. R. Ackroyd, C. F. E., 1970. The Cambridge History of the Bible, Volume 1. In: *The Cambridge History of the Bible, Volume 1*. Cambridge: Cambridge University Press, p. 305.

[51] Redd, N. T., 2017. *How Big is the Universe?*. [Online] Available at: https://www.space.com/24073-how-big-is-the-universe.html

[52] Redd, N. T., 2017. *How Big is the Universe?*. [Online] Available at: https://www.space.com/24073-how-big-is-the-universe.html

[53] Redd, N. T., 2018. *Space.com*. [Online] Available at: https://www.space.com/15830-light-speed.html

[54] Sharp, T., 2017. *How Far is Earth from the Sun?*. [Online] Available at: https://www.space.com/17081-how-far-is-earth-from-the-sun.html

[55] McClure, B., 2018. *How far is a light-year?*. [Online] Available at: https://earthsky.org/astronomy-essentials/how-far-is-a-light-year

[56] Lumen, n.d. *Animal Reproduction and Development*. [Online] Available at: https://courses.lumenlearning.com/boundless-biology/chapter/reproduction-methods/

[57] Sharp, T., 2017. *How Far is Earth from the Sun?*. [Online] Available at: https://www.space.com/17081-how-far-is-earth-from-the-sun.html

[58] Crace, J., 2005. *Michio Kaku: Mr. Parallel Universe*. [Online] Available at: https://www.theguardian.com/education/2005/feb/22/highereducation.highereducationprofile

[59] Mark, J. J., 2017. *Ancient Egyptian Law*. [Online] Available at: https://www.ancient.eu/Egyptian_Law/

[60] Roth, M., 1995. Law Collections from Mesopotamia and Asia Minor. In: *Law Collections from Mesopotamia and Asia Minor.* Atlanta: Society of Biblical Literature, pp. 13-22.

[61] Mason, M., 2008. *Burned at the Stake for Believing in Science.* [Online] Available at: http://discovermagazine.com/2008/sep/06-burned-at-the-stake-for-believing-in-science

[62] Foxearth & District Local History Society, n.d. *The Swimming of Witches.* [Online] Available at: http://www.foxearth.org.uk/SwimmingOfWitches.html

[63] Donatella Lippi, D. W., 2012. Witchcraft, Medicine and Society in Early Modern Europe. In: *Witchcraft, Medicine and Society in Early Modern Europe.* Florence: University of Florence, pp. 68-73.

[64] (Paraphrased from Luther's "Against the Robbing and Murdering Hordes of Peasants" 1525)

[65] Americans United for Separation of Church and State, 2019. *Is America A Christian Nation?.* [Online] Available at: https://www.au.org/resources/publications/is-america-a-christian-nation

[66] Thakkar, C., 2015. *Karma.* [Online] Available at: https://www.ancient.eu/Karma/

[67] Dooling, D. M., 1987. The Sons of the Wind: the Sacred Stories of the Lakota. In: *The Sons of the Wind: the Sacred Stories of the Lakota.* New York: Parabola Books, p. 136.

[68] Powers, W. K., 1977. Oglala Religion. In: *Oglala Religion.* Lincoln/London: University of Nebraska Press, p. 233.

[69] Stanford Encyclopedia of Philosophy, 2010. *African Ethics.* [Online] Available at: https://plato.stanford.edu/entries/african-ethics/

[70] Bradshaw, S., 2003. *Vatican: condoms don't stop Aids.* [Online] Available at: https://www.theguardian.com/world/2003/oct/09/aids

[71] DART, R. C. a. J., 1989. RELIGION CATHOLICS : Bishops' Panel Rejects Condoms in AIDS Battle. *Los Angeles Times*, 13 October.

[72] U.S. Catholic, 2019. *Where there is pain, there is God.* [Online] Available at: https://www.uscatholic.org/articles/201602/where-there-pain-there-god-30557

[73] Johnson, T. M. G. A. Z. A. W. H. a. P. F. C., 2015. Christianity 2015: Religious Diversity and Personal Contact. *International Bulletin of Missionary Research Vol. 39, no. 1*, 28 January, pp. 28-29.

[74] (James 1:1)

[75] (Deut. 7:6)

[76] (Acts 3:25)

[77] (Mark 8:36)

[78] (1 Timothy 6:10)

[79] (MATT 7:1)

[80] (Rev. 21:8)

[81] (Rev. 22:11)

[82] Smithsonian Institute, 2019. *What does it mean to be human?.* [Online] Available at: http://humanorigins.si.edu/evidence/genetics

[83] Daley, J., 2017. *Genetic Study Shows Skin Color Is Only Skin Deep.* [Online] Available at: https://www.smithsonianmag.com/smart-news/genetic-study-shows-skin-color-just-skin-deep-180965261/

[84] Rice University, 2019. *Anatomy and Physiology - Layers of the Skin.* [Online] Available at: https://opentextbc.ca/anatomyandphysiology/chapter/5-1-layers-of-the-skin/

[85] Heather Brannon, M., 2018. *The Individual Layers of Skin and Their Functions.* [Online] Available at: https://www.verywellhealth.com/skin-anatomy-1068880

[86] Lohnes, K., 2018. *Siege of Jerusalem.* [Online] Available at: https://www.britannica.com/event/Siege-of-Jerusalem-70

[87] Matthews, R., 2017. *Sack of Constantinople.* [Online] Available at: https://www.britannica.com/event/Sack-of-Constantinople-1204

[88] Haughton, B., 2011. *What happened to the Great Library at Alexandria?.*

[Online] Available at: https://www.ancient.eu/article/207/what-happened-to-the-great-library-at-alexandria/

[89] McKernan, B., 2016. *Isis 'destroys thousands of years of culture almost overnight' as it flees Iraqi army near Mosul.* [Online] Available at: https://www.independent.co.uk/news/world/middle-east/isis-mosul-iraq-army-terrorists-destroy-demolish-nimrud-temples-artefacts-a7418136.html

[90] Higgins, E. S., 2017. *Is Mental Health Declining in the U.S.?* [Online] Available at: https://www.scientificamerican.com/article/is-mental-health-declining-in-the-u-s/

[91] Health Direct, 2019. *Causes of mental illness.* [Online] Available at: https://www.healthdirect.gov.au/causes-of-mental-illness

[92] Cafasso, J., 2018. *Chemical Imbalance in the Brain: What You Should Know.* [Online] Available at: https://www.healthline.com/health/chemical-imbalance-in-the-brain#causes

[93] Demographic Partitions, 2017. *5 Most Celebrated Holidays around the World.* [Online] Available at: http://demographicpartitions.org/5-celebrated-holidays-around-world/

[94] Time and Date, 1995-2019. *TimeandDate.com.* [Online] Available at: https://www.timeanddate.com/calendar/gregorian-calendar.html

[95] Colagrossi, M., 2018. *How Christians co-opted the winter solstice.* [Online] Available at: https://bigthink.com/culture-religion/how-christians-co-opted-the-winter-solstice?rebelltitem=2#rebelltitem2

[96] Eldridge, A., 2019. *7 Winter Solstice Celebrations From Around the World.* [Online] Available at: https://www.britannica.com/list/7-winter-solstice-celebrations-from-around-the-world

[97] BARBOZA, D., 2008. *In Chinese Factories, Lost Fingers and Low Pay.* [Online] Available at: https://www.nytimes.com/2008/01/05/business/worldbusiness/05sweatshop.html

[98] Union of Concerned Scientists, 2019. *The Hidden Costs of Fossil Fuels.* [Online] Available at: https://www.ucsusa.org/clean-energy/coal-and-other-fossil-fuels/hidden-cost-of-fossils#.XFj5PPZFzIU

Made in the USA
Columbia, SC
07 September 2023

22590538R00171